Analyzing the Grammar of English

A Brief Undergraduate Textbook

Second Edition

Analyzing the Grammar of English

A BRIEF UNDERGRADUATE TEXTBOOK

Second Edition

Richard V. Teschner and Eston Evans

GEORGETOWN UNIVERSITY PRESS/WASHINGTON, D.C.

Georgetown University Press, Washington, D.C.

10   9   8   7   6   5   4   3   2   1   2000

This volume is printed on acid-free offset book paper.

Library of Congress Cataloging-in-Publication Data

Teschner, Richard V.
    Analyzing the grammer of English : a brief undergraduate textbook / Richard V.
    Teschner, Eston Evans.—2nd ed.
        p.   cm.
    Includes index.
    ISBN 0-87840-807-X (pbk. : alk. paper)
        1. English language—Grammar.   I. Evans, Eston.   II. Title.

PE1112.T48 2000
425—dc21   00-023275

TABLE OF CONTENTS

3: BASIC STRUCTURES, QUESTIONS, *DO*-INSERTION, NEGATION, AUXILIARIES, RESPONSES, EMPHASIS, CONTRACTION   77

4: MODALS. PREPOSITIONAL AND PARTICLE VERBS. TRANSITIVITY AND VOICE. CONDITIONALITY.   107

7: ADVERBS. IT AND THERE: REFERENTIALS AND NON-REFERENTIALS. CLEFTS.   251

8: COMPOUND SENTENCES: COORDINATION, SUBORDINATION   277

INTRODUCTION

Analyzing the Grammar of English: A Brief Undergraduate Textbook (AGE:BUT) is precisely what its title implies: an analysis of the grammar of a particular language (English), not an introduction to linguistics whose examples happen to be English-derived; a textbook, not a complete reference grammar; and a brief treatise, one which the authors' classroom experience has shown to be completable in full in a 15-week semester. As a brief, introductory, undergraduate textbook, AGE:BUT keeps footnotes to a bare minimum and makes no attempt at bibliographical coverage. On the other hand, exercises abound and make up the heart of the work.

Though not intended solely as a pedagogical grammar, AGE:BUT has been used successfully with advanced ESOL students as a combination review grammar and first course in the analysis of English as a grammatical system. AGE:BUT's main target populations are persons majoring in English, linguistics, or linguistics' allied or ancillary disciplines (such as the many subfields of Education) for whom a course in English grammatical analysis forms part of the curriculum.

ANALYZING ENGLISH

Ways of Analyzing a Language

Analyzing a language means taking it apart to see what makes it work. We can analyze the sounds of a language. We can perform an analysis of the units that convey meaning at the level of the word, the phrase, the clause, the sentence, or even beyond. We can analyze the order in which words appear. Analyzing a language can also involve discussing the sort of language variation that is determined by one's region, one's social class, one's age, one's ethnic background, and even one's sex, one's generation, or the quality of education one has had.

Under normal conditions, children control the grammar of the language of their home and their neighborhood at a relatively young age. What exactly is the grammar that these budding speakers acquire with such amazing proficiency that they give the impression of handling it with little apparent effort? Essentially this grammar consists of a combination of elements which convey meaning; these elements include **sounds** (phonetics and phonology), **words** (the lexicon), **words' constituent elements** (morphology), the **arrangement of words into phrases, clauses, and sentences** (syntax), **intonation and stress** (prosody), and the **overall ability to apply all these appropriately in a given situation** (pragmatics).

Children rarely analyze their language in any formal way, at least not before they are told to do so by language-conscious parents and instructors. In school, teachers go about polishing children's language skills—mainly reading and writing—and admonish them almost constantly to monitor their language and to use it "properly." This level of language analysis is known as **prescriptive grammar**; when working from textbooks in prescriptive grammar, children are expected to impose conscious rules of language usage on the unanalyzed language they already speak fluently. Prescriptive grammarians often expect children to change the way they speak. Children are told that to avoid being stigmatized as uneducated by using "bad grammar," they must learn and conform to certain standards that are said to typify the language of the most prestigious adult speakers of their wider speech community.

Another form of language analysis is known as **descriptive grammar**, and it is this type of language analysis that informs the present textbook.

Descriptive grammar presents the facts about a language as it is actually spoken in a systematic, non-judgmental fashion. Analyzing grammar in this fashion requires us to consider all utterances in English by any native speaker of English to be grammatical, i.e., well-formed. In doing so, we ignore temporarily the fact that all native speakers of all ages make occasional **performance errors** or slips of the tongue in such areas as word choice, structure, or pronunciation; these performance errors are caused by such inadvertent factors as haste, tension, fatigue, inattention, or inebriation, or by deliberate attempts to use the language in a humorous or ironic way.

One example of the way descriptive analysis works is the way it deals with English sounds. For instance, almost all native speakers of English produce and comprehend such rapidly spoken utterances as "Jeet jet?" or "Sko!" ('Did you eat yet?' and 'Let's go!', respectively). A prescriptive grammarian would simply condemn these utterances out of hand, whereas a descriptive grammarian seeks to describe the conditions under which they are produced and the phonetic processes by which "Did you eat yet?" gets changed into "Jeet jet?" In similar fashion, descriptivists perform analysis on language units at the level of the word, the phrase, the clause, the sentence, or even the entire discourse or conversation. Words, for instance, can take on different forms to serve different functions: *murder* (noun/verb), *murdered* (past-tense or past participle verb form), *murderous* (adjective), *murderously* (adverb). Through descriptive analysis we are able to recognize how word order affects meaning, as in the phrases *only a child* and *an only child* or in the sentences "We just had the house painted" and "We had just painted the house." Descriptive analysis helps in revealing and explaining the meaning of seemingly nonsensical yet perfectly grammatical sentences such as "The old man the boats" and "The horse raced past the barn fell."

Literate speakers of English (be they native speakers, native-like speakers, near-natives in fact, or near-natives in training) who have an interest in language and who intend to teach English language arts or English to Speakers of Other Languages (ESOL) will find this textbook valuable and challenging, or so we hope. This book should prove helpful in enabling you to gain systematic insight into how language works.

EXERCISE 1.1

(A) Consider the following nonsense sentences:

1. It's cliggy to spip a rozer in stram.
2. Colorless green ideas sleep furiously.

Although these sentences communicate no meaning or seem to be quite contradictory, they nonetheless sound grammatical. Why? Try replacing the nonsensical or contradictory elements so that the sentences make sense.

(B) Pretend that you are a nit-picking prescriptive grammarian of the old school. Which of the following sentences would you consider unacceptable? Do you consider some of them to be acceptable in speech but not in writing? What changes, if any, would you make in these sentences?

1. Him and me was gonna buy one a dem new video games.

2. Did you hear about Sally and I? We're history.

3. Joe don't like me no more.

4. She sure is pretty, ain't she?

5. Folks drive real friendly in Texas.

6. Where's the books I put here a minute ago?

(C) Change the following rapidly pronounced English utterances into standard English orthography (spelling).

1. Hoozat?

2. Werezeeat? — Heezupeer.

3. Gotneebread?

4. I spoze.

(D) Rewrite the following fully grammatical sentences so that they are easier to understand.

1. That's the cheese the rat the cat caught ate.

2. The boy the woman heard shout left.

(E) How many different meanings does each of the following sentences have?

1. He fed her dog biscuits.

2. The shooting of the hunters occurred at dawn.

3. Visiting relatives should be outlawed.

Parts of Speech

All words in any language can be classified as to how they function. English is no exception to this rule. English words (and phrases) are thus variously categorizable as nouns, adjectives, pronouns, verbs, adverbs, determiners, prepositions, conjunctions and so forth. The following definitions are deliberately brief and simple, and will be expanded upon throughout the rest of AGE:BUT.

NOUN

According to one well-known meaning-based or **semantic** definition, a noun is 'a concept, person, place or thing.' However, nouns are both more and less than that. Since many words ordinarily belonging to non-noun part-of-speech categories can be **nominalized** ('made to function like nouns'), defining **noun** can be rather like defining water: you find it almost everywhere. But a noun, like H_2O, has certain properties which we can specify by means of applying various tests. One such test asks whether a given word can fit in the blank that appears in the following exercise. (If it can, it's a noun.)

EXERCISE 1.2

(A) Tell which of the words below can appear in the blank space in the following environment:

I saw $\begin{bmatrix} \text{the} \\ \text{a} \\ \text{some} \\ \emptyset \end{bmatrix}$ _____ .

1. never	13. next
2. horse	14. contradiction
3. sand	15. apple
4. children	16. gastroenterologist
5. from	17. smiled
6. gave	18. shrink
7. grave	19. shrank
8. any	20. cheese
9. brick	21. Suzie
10. bombing	22. Madrid
11. somewhere	23. ghost
12. blond	24. honorable

Another way to determine if something is a noun is to ask whether the genitive case's **possessive marker** /z/ (usually spelled 's or s') can be attached to the end of it. Only nouns can co-occur with the possessive /z/: the boy's mother, a building's infrastructure, the teachers' salaries (but *the from's family, *a killed's weapon, *the quickly's performance). (Note that in linguistic analysis, an asterisk— * —is placed immediately before anything that is **ungrammatical**, i.e., anything that no native speaker would ever say except as a joke or as a slip of the tongue. **Ungrammatical** is **NOT** the same as stigmatized, which means 'not generally accepted'. "Not generally accepted" refers to anything that some or many native speakers do indeed say but other native speakers disapprove of. Examples of stigmatized usage are words like ain't and irregardless or sentences like Him 'n' me would of did it real good, which may sound bad to you but which **is** said by native speakers of English and which **does** convey meaning. An example of **ungrammatical** usage is this: *Him book the tomorrow give she to is. [An experienced teacher might be able to decipher this as seeking to mean "She is to give him the book tomorrow."]) A third test for whether something is a noun is whether a given word can co-occur with the /z/ that marks pluralization. (This /z/ is typically spelled -s or -es.) Again, only a noun can so co-occur: the dogs, the tables, some solutions (but *the overs, *many chosens, *fourteen strenuouslies).

VERB

From a semantic standpoint, verbs serve several purposes: to **equate** X with Y ("Joe is a language teacher"); to indicate **state or condition** ("Joe seems sick today," "Joe looks very weak"); and to indicate the **performance of action** ("Joe grades ten sets of papers every month"). Most verbs indicate the performance of action. Yet other verbs are often used as **auxiliaries,** i.e., they are followed by other verb forms—the **lexical verbs**—which carry the main semantic content of the phrase: "Joe has purchased 26 cases of beer for the party." "Joe will feel sick tomorrow." Only verbs can be **conjugated** ('undergo the alterations brought about by changing into different tenses, persons and numbers'); thus only a verb can take the English past-tense marker -ed (stay → stayed, kill → killed, snore → snored), whereas other parts of speech can not (sofa → *sofaed, very → *veryed, nothing → *nothinged).

ADJECTIVE

A semantic characterisic of adjectives is that they **describe, modify, distinguish or otherwise characterize** the noun they refer to. Here are some examples: "The ugly baboon stole the cute little monkey's banana"; "They were both killed by an evil green monster"; "You'll find tremendous bargains at the new supermarket." As regards **form,** many (but not all) adjectives take the **comparative and superlative suffixes** -er and -est respectively; thus: new → newer → newest; ugly → uglier → ugliest. Other adjectives form compara-

tives and superlatives by appearing after the words more or most: evil →
more evil → most evil; tremendous → more tremendous → most tremendous.

ADVERB

Adverbs are to verbs as adjectives are to nouns. The adverb modifies, char-
acterizes or otherwise attributes a **manner** to its verb: "Connie jumped up
quickly and ran away frantically" ('in a quick manner', 'in a frantic manner'). Adverbs also function as **intensifiers** modifying adjectives ("Joe is a
very hard-working scholar"), as intensifiers modifying other adverbs ("Joe
works very rapidly"), and even as modifiers of entire sentences, as in the
following: "Clearly ['It is clear that'] you want me to leave"; "I will leave
tomorrow ['It is tomorrow when I will leave']."

PRONOUN

"Pro" + "noun" typically means 'in place of, instead of' a noun or a noun
phrase. Pronouns, then, replace nouns ("Joe was tired, so he [Joe] went
home"), but pronouns can also refer back to nouns as well ("Joe told Geri
that he wanted her to get him a hot water bottle"). In addition, pronouns
can stand for a referent that actually lacks a noun antecedent: "I saw you in
the swimming pool"; "Will somebody please help me?" Pronouns can be
personal (I/me, you/you, he/him, . . .), **reflexive** (myself, yourself, . . .),
possessive pronominals (mine, yours, his, . . .), **reciprocal** (each other),
relative/interrogative (who, which, what, whose, where, when, that, . . .),
demonstrative (this [one], that [one], . . .), or **indefinite** (someone, . . .).

DETERMINER

A determiner is either an **article**—(**definite**) the, or (**indefinite**) a/an,
some—, a **demonstrative** (this, these, that, those), or a possessive (my, your,
his, her, its, our, their).

QUANTIFIER

Quantifiers indicate the relative amount or quantity of whatever the following noun denotes. Quantifiers (and unit words) occur immediately before
or after articles or demonstratives that head up noun phrases: many fail-
ures, many of the children, much effort, lots of paper, few elephants, gallons
of dirty polluted water.

PREPOSITION

Prepositions are "short" or "little" words which express relationships
including those of space, time and degree. The 20 most common English

prepositions are (in alphabetical order): at, about, above, against, around, before, below, between, by, for, from, in, of, on, over, through, to, toward(s), under, and with. Here are some examples of prepositions expressing: **spatial relationship** ("French is spoken in France, Belgium, Switzerland, Québec and elsewhere"); **time** ("I'll meet you at 3 p.m."); **degree** ("He weighs about 400 pounds").

Not covered in this encapsulated presentation of English parts of speech are: **conjunctions** (and, but, or, nor) as well as **complementizers** (that, as, for . . . to, than, if and others). See ch. 8 for a thorough presentation of conjunctions and complementizers.

EXERCISE 1.3

(A) Tell whether the underlined words are nouns, verbs, adjectives, adverbs, pronouns, determiners, quantifiers, or prepositions.

1. The architect protested that someone was changing his plans.
       1   2   3   4   5   6   7 8

2. I told him he should give me the foreign money immediately.
    1 2 3   4   5   6   7   8   9

3. Apparently someone grabbed my purse and threw me to the ground.
       1   2   3   4   5 6 7   8 9 10   11

4. That man told me many different versions of the old legend that
     1   2   3   4   5   6   7   8 9 10   11   12

   his Armenian grandfather remembered.
   13   14   15   16

5. Yesterday they tried several different approaches but none
        1   2   3   4   5   6   7

   worked.
     8

6. The mayor has tons of money he deposited in various banks
     1   2   3   4 5   6 7   8   9   10   11

   around the world.
     12   13   14

Cases

Two parts of speech—nouns, pronouns—are used in different **cases** depending on the function they have. Thus if a noun/pronoun (n/p) is doing the action in the sentence, that n/p is in the **subject** case, and if a "subject" form of the n/p exists, then that's the form we use. Another way to determine which word is the subject is to look for it at the beginning of the sentence or the clause, where English subjects usually occur. Here are several examples: "John loves Marsha. However, Marsha doesn't love John." (In the first sentence, John is the subject, but in the second sentence, Marsha is the subject.) Yet another way to pick out the **subject** is to look for the word that sometimes changes the form of the verb. For example, because one pronoun, I, takes the verb form leave ("I leave home every morning at 8") while another pronoun, she, takes a different verb form (leaves, as in "She leaves home every morning at 7:45"), we conclude that both I and she function as **subjects**.

Other English noun or pronoun cases are the **object** case and the **genitive** case. The object case n/p receives the action of the verb, while the genitive case n/p indicates possession, i.e., who owns something.

Here are some examples of each case—genitive, object, and subject:

GENITIVE CASE

Sarah's mother is my father's cousin.
The store's hours are from 7 a.m. to 11 p.m.
The horses' legs were broken because of the two riders' negligence.

As you can see, nouns in the genitive case are marked by either 's or s'. The apostrophe is always used. Because of that, we can usually spot a genitive case. (Rule of thumb: if a noun ends in 's or s', it's in the genitive case; if it does not, it's in some other case.)

OBJECT CASE AND SUBJECT CASE

English **nouns** that are functioning as objects have the same form as nouns that are functioning as subjects.

Sue saw Sarah at the seashore.
Sarah greeted Sue effusively.

The factory employs many people.
Many people leave the factory when the whistle blows.

However, most English **pronouns** functioning as objects do **not** have the same forms as pronouns functioning as subjects. Here are some examples; the ones sharing different forms are underlined:

—subject pronouns

I   you   he   she   it   we   they

—object pronouns

me   you   him   her   it   us   them

For more information about case, see p. 161.

EXERCISE 1.4

(A) Tell whether the underlined words are genitives, objects or subjects.

1. <u>They</u> told <u>me</u> <u>the secret</u>.

2. <u>Joe</u> found <u>Sandy's</u> notes in the library.

3. <u>He</u> later told <u>me</u> that <u>he</u> had destroyed <u>them</u>.

4. <u>Fifteen desperately ill graduate students</u> arrived late

5. Only <u>two candidates</u> mailed <u>us</u> <u>the right material</u>.

6. <u>Anne Marie</u> initially told <u>Bea</u> <u>the truth</u>.

7. <u>She</u> subsequently told <u>her</u> <u>a terrible bunch of lies</u>.

Word Order / Syntax

Most non-compound sentences can be described by a series of what are known as **phrase structure rules**. In these rules (here presented in simplified form), abbreviations are used: thus s represents **sentence**, np **noun phrase**, vp **verb phrase**, pp **prepositional phrase**, n **noun**, v **verb**, and so forth.

Here is a typical phrase structure rule:

s →np vp

We read the rule thus:

"A sentence consists of a noun phrase first and a verb phrase next."

What follow are some sentences that conform to this rule; their components are identified.

1. Judy screamed.
   np   vp

2. My sister Judy screamed loudly.
   np   vp

3. The quick brown fox jumped over the lazy sleeping dog.
   np   vp

That the **norm** in English is s → np vp and not *s → vp np can be proven by the following ungrammatical sentences:

4. *Screamed Judy.
5. *Screamed loudly my sister Judy.
6. *Jumped over the lazy sleeping dog the quick brown fox.

Word order can also be established for the individual **components** of both np and vp; thus:

$$np \rightarrow \begin{bmatrix} \text{(det) (adj) n} \\ \\ \text{pro} \end{bmatrix}$$

(**det** = determiner)
(**adj** = adjective)
(**pro** = pronoun)

This equation means that <u>np</u> can consist of five possibilities:

1. men
   n

2. those men
   det   n

3. angry men
   adj   n

4. those angry men
   det   adj   n

5. they
   pro

Likewise, <u>vps</u> lend themselves to a (simplified) phrase structure rule:

$$vp \rightarrow \begin{bmatrix} be & \begin{bmatrix} np \\ ap \\ pp \end{bmatrix} \\ v\ (np)\ (pp) \end{bmatrix}$$

(**np** = noun phrase)
(**ap** = adjective phrase)
(**pp** = prepositional phrase)

Since square brackets require us to choose one element from within them, while elements within parentheses are **optional** ('can be chosen but do not have to be'), vp can consist of seven different sentence types:

1. Wanda is a doctor.
   BE np

2. Wanda is rich.
   BE ap

3. Wanda is in Beverly Hills.
   BE pp

4. Wanda runs.
   v

5. Wanda runs for her life.
   v   pp

6. Wanda runs a clinic.
   v   np

7. Wanda runs a clinic for rich neurotics.
   v   np   pp

In similar fashion, ap and pp lend themselves to a more thorough description by means of phrase structure rules:

ap → (intens) adj (pp)   (**intens** = intensifier—words such as very, highly, slightly, somewhat . . .)

1. Vito is interested.
   adj
2. Vito is interested in his boss's daughter.
   adj   underline{pp}
3. Vito is very interested.
   intens   adj
4. Vito is very interested in his boss's daughter.
   intens   adj   underline{pp}

Phrase structure rules can also be established for <u>pp</u>s:

pp → p np

1. Hsu is in the garden.
   p   np
      \ /
       pp
2. Hsu bought collard greens at the supermarket.
            p   np
               \ /
                pp
3. Hsu was chosen employee of the month.
            p   np
               \ /
                pp

EXERCISE 1.5

(A) In the blank spaces on the left, write in full the phrase structure that describes each of the following sentences.

_____   **1.** Lisa talked on the phone.

_____   **2.** Newt was a congressman.

_____   **3.** Elvis sang songs of love.

_____   **4.** Richie Valens died in a plane crash.

_____   **5.** Peggy Sue married her boyfriend in a beautiful ceremony.

_____   **6.** I want the biggest car on the lot.

_____   **7.** The lazy fox kissed the tired old princess.

_____   **8.** Jean was extremely nervous about the test.

_____   **9.** The butler killed the chambermaid in the library.

10. Gremlins are very vicious.

Sounds: Phonemes and Allophones

When we discuss the sounds of a language, we need to know about any differences that may exist between its **phonemes** and its **allophones**.

A **phoneme** is an abstract representation of a sound or of several sounds. An **allophone** is the actual sound itself. The following example will illustrate the difference between phonemes and allophones: American English contains four sounds which are similar but not identical in the way they are pronounced and in the way they sound: the [tʰ] of tell ([tʰɛl]), the [t] of style ([stail]), the [t⁻] of wait ([wet⁻]), and the [D] of waiting ([wé-DIŋ]). Each of these four—[tʰ t t⁻ D]—possesses a different sound and thus qualifies as a different allophone. However, if we substitute one of these allophones for another, we do not change the meaning of the word; thus a [t] rather than a [tʰ] in a word like tell (mispronounced [tɛl]) may sound funny, foreign-accented, or not normal in some other way, but it still gives us the sequence of sounds that speakers of English automatically associate with the definition 'communicate information to someone' ("She will tell him the truth tomorrow"). However, if we substitute an [s] for our [tʰ], then the meaning of the sequence changes completely, since [sɛl] is the result, as in "She will sell him the truth tomorrow"). Because [s] and [t] when substituted for each other will often change the meaning of the word, we say that /s/ and /t/ are not only different allophones but also **different abstract units of sound which serve to distinguish meaning**. Such abstract units are called **phonemes**. When a sound has the status of a phoneme, its substitution for another phoneme will often change the meaning of a sequence of sounds, as the sell/tell example has shown and as the following will show as well:

[sel]	sail	vs.	[tel]	tail
[nis]	niece	vs.	[nit]	neat
[bɛs]	Bess	vs.	[bɛl]	bel
[soil]	soil	vs	[toil]	toil

In most of the world's written languages the relationship between the sound system (**phonology**) and the spelling system (**orthography**) is not a perfect one. The phonology/orthography relationship is known as **fit**. If a written language enjoys **perfect fit**, then each individual phoneme is spelled with just one particular **grapheme** ('letter of the alphabet'); and, conversely, each particular grapheme represents just one individual phoneme. Perfect fit means a one-on-one relationship: for each grapheme, just one phoneme, and for each phoneme, just one grapheme.

English orthography's fit is not especially good. To a great extent that is due to the following fact: while in most varieties of English there are **twelve vowel phonemes**, the English alphabet contains only **five vowel graphemes**. Thus the potential for inconsistency and mismatch was high to begin with. Here are just two examples of that inconsistency:

ENGLISH VOWEL PHONEME	GRAPHEMES USED TO REPRESENT IT	
/i/	ee	see
	ea	sea
	ie	niece
	ei	perceive
	e	scene
	ey	key
	eo	people
	i	Geraldine
	y	happy

/u/	oo	soon
	ou	group
	u	cute
	ui	suit
	o	move
	wo	two
	ough	through
	ew	grew

Since English orthography's fit is not especially good, and because the findings of phonological analysis have not been widely disseminated until recently, many elementary school and high school textbooks continue to follow an antiquated and thoroughly discredited tradition whereby terms such as "long" and "short" are used to differentiate between English vowel phonemes. For example, your own elementary school teacher may have spoken of the "long a as in hate vs. the short a as in fact" or words to that effect. Terms such as "long" and "short" should never be used when describing English vowel phonemes. Instead, linguistics has come up with terms that precisely describe the part of the mouth where each vowel is articulated. These terms involve words such as **closed, mid, open, front, central, back** and others which you are about to learn. Use is also made of **transcriptional symbols** to represent sounds. These symbols belong to something called the **IPA**—the **International Phonetic Alphabet**—which was invented in the 1880s in order to provide a consistent and universally accepted system for **transcribing** ('writing out') the sounds of any language. So when linguists wish to refer, for example, to the sound produced by the grapheme *a* in the word hate, they can either **describe** it using the terms ("mid front tense vowel") that we are about to learn, or else they can **transcribe** it using this symbol: /e/. (Phoneme /e/—whose only allophone in English is [e]—represents the mid front tense vowel and only that vowel.)

In the paragraphs that follow, our goal is not to present a complete description of the allophones of English and how they are articulated, nor to follow that with an analysis of their various distinctive features. Instead, analysis begins at the phoneme level and is kept as brief as our purpose allows.

English has 12 vowel phonemes in most dialects and 25 consonant phonemes in nearly all dialects. All English vowel phonemes are **voiced**. This means that the **vocal cords** vibrate during the articulation of the sound. This vibration is called a **coarticulatory feature** because it takes place at the same time. Vocal cord vibration accompanies the articulation of any voiced sound. To prove this, place several fingers over your larynx (Adam's apple) and pronounce these two words:

    bus   buzz

In buzz (/bʌz/), the vocal cords will vibrate from the beginning of the word through the end of it, while in bus (/bʌs/), vibration will occur only for the /b/ and the /ʌ/ but not for the /s/.

English vowels are distributed in a more or less **quadrangular** manner—on a vowel **quadrangle,** so to speak, for which please see the following chart. The six descriptors on the chart—front/central/back and closed/mid/open—refer to the part of the mouth where the vowel is pronounced. For **closed vowels** (/i I u ʊ/), the blade of the tongue is close to the roof of the mouth, for **open vowels** (/æ ɔ a/), the tongue is depressed, leaving the mouth "open" with a maximum amount of space between tongue blade and mouth roof; for **mid vowels** (/e ɛ o ɔ ʌ ə/), the tongue's position is somewhere in between these two extremes.

The following chart presents the English vowel phonemes.

THE TWELVE ENGLISH VOWEL PHONEMES

		front	central	back		
closed	tense	i			u	tense	closed
	lax	I		U	lax
mid	tense	e		o	tense	mid
			ə ʌ	
	lax	ɛ		ɔ	lax
open		æ	a			open

As compared, for example, to Spanish, English has exactly twice as many closed front, mid front, closed back, and mid back vowels; this is because all English vowels in these four categories are either **tense** or **lax**, a distinction that languages like Spanish never make. A **tense vowel** is not only articulated with greater muscular tension (hence its name), but, more importantly, a tense vowel comes close to being a **diphthong**. (A **diphthong** is a single-syllable combination of two closed vowels, or of one closed and one non-closed vowel.) When a tense vowel is articulated, the tongue begins a bit low but changes position, gliding upward towards the roof of the mouth. Thus phoneme /i/ is phonetically something like [ɪy], a sound which begins lower in the mouth than the [i] of Spanish, French, German, and other languages, but ends up higher than [i] with the tongue practically touching the **palate** ('roof of the mouth').

Since English has so many vowel phonemes, it is forced to use some strange-looking IPA symbols to represent some of them. Thus the symbols for all four lax vowels—ɪ ɛ ʊ ɔ—are either unconventional or rare, as are the symbols /æ ʌ ə/. To relate symbols to sounds, you should learn the following sound-to-symbol equivalencies (accompanied by example words that illustrate the particular vowel sound):

front	central	back
/i/ beet		/u/ boot
/I/ bit		/ʊ/ book
	/ə/ above	
/e/ bait	/ʌ/ above	/o/ boat
/ɛ/ bet		/ɔ/ bought
/æ/ bat		/a/ father

One extremely important characteristic of English is that it reduces vowels. English is a **vowel-reducing** language. This means that **ALL UNSTRESSED VOWELS HAVE THE SAME ESSENTIAL SOUND**, the /ə/, which is called the **schwa**. The /ə/ is represented on our charts as mid-central and thus acoustically similar to the /ʌ/, whose name is **chevron**. Sometimes /ə/ indeed sounds just like /ʌ/, as in the word above /əb ʌ́v/, but sometimes /ə/ is better described as something closer to lax front closed /I/. In colloquial or rapid speech, reduction of unstressed English vowels appearing before the consonants /n m l r/ can go even further, to the point where the vowel disappears altogether, leaving the consonant as the **nucleus of the syllable**. When the consonants /n m l r/ serve as **syllabic nucleii**, they are written with short vertical lines beneath them, thus: n̩ m̩ l̩ r̩. We thus pronounce the word edification as /ɛ̀-dì-fə-ké-šən/ when we speak at a slow and careful rate of speed, but as /ɛ̀-də-fə-ké-šn̩/ when we speak rapidly. Note the use of **diacritics** in these transcriptions. The diacritics—the various accent marks—indicate degrees of stress. Thus the acute accent— ´ —indicates **strong stress**, the grave accent— ` —indicates **weak stress.** When no diacritic appears, no stress is present. "Stress" in English and most other languages refers to **vocal emphasis** and involves any of the following phenomena, alone or in combination: **pitch** (like notes on a musical scale, which can be high, low, or in between); **volume** ('loudness', i.e., how loud the sound segment is); and **length** (i.e., how much time is spent articulating the sound segment).

English has only three actual **diphthongs**, all beginning with a back vowel sound. The diphthongs are:

/oi/	soil, boy
/au/	house, cow
/ai/	high, try, die

As we have already indicated, English has 25 **consonant phonemes**. In the consonant phoneme chart that follows, voiceless consonants appear on the top line, voiced consonants on the bottom. Note that there are eight voiceless/voiced pairs in English:

voiceless	p	f	θ	t	s	š	č	k
voiced	b	v	ð	d	z	ž	ǰ	g

Here is the consonant chart:

ENGLISH CONSONANT PHONEMES

voiceless	p	f		θ	t s		š č		k	ʍ h
voiced	b m w v			ð	d z n l		ž ǰ	r j	g	ŋ

Some of these phoneme symbols need exemplification:

/θ/	think, with, ether
/ð/	these, loathe, either
/š/	shell, wish, champagne
/č/	church, choose, witch
/ž/	measure, rouge, pleasure
/ǰ/	judge, jury, George
/j/	young, youthful, Yale
/ŋ/	sing, tingle, ringing, wrinkle
/ʍ/	when, whether, while

EXERCISE 1.6

(A) Write out these sentences in standard English orthography.

1. /ðə-kwĭk-bráun-fáks-jʌ̀mpt-ó-vṛ-ðə-lé-zì-slí-pĭŋ-dɔ́g/

2. /àid-lʌ́v-tù-gó-àn-ə-wɔ́k-wĭθ-jù/
/bʌ̀t-àim-vé-rì-bí-zì-jʌ̀st-nàu/

3. /ší-sóld-sí-šèlz-ænd-rúž-bài-ðə-sí-šòr/
/tù-čár-ḷz-brʌ́-ðṛ-jĭm/ /ænd-sév- rəl-fréndz-əv-hĭz/

4. /wì-nú-jù-tʊ́k-ə-bʊ́k-tù-lúk-ænd-sú/
/bʌ̀t-ðè-dĭd-ṇt-hæv-ə-čǽns-tù-ríd-ĭt-θrú/

5. /pɔ́l-pʊ́št-pæt-ʌ́n-dṛ-ðə-pír-ænd-nír -lì-dráund-hṛ/

6. /ʍĭč-wʌ́n-əv-jú-wánts-tə-mé-žṛ-ðæ̀t-θĭn-jʌ́ŋ-krá-kə-dàilz-nóz/

7. /æn-ɔ́-fḷ-smél-ròz-ʌ́p-frʌ̀m-ðə-pĭgz-trɔ́f/
/æ̀f-tṛ-jórǰ-θrù-ĭn-ə-rát-ṇ-bə-nǽ-nə/

8. /ʍái-dĭd-ðə-káu-kĭk-ðə-bói-ĭn-hĭz-héd/

(B) Write out these words in phonemic transcription.

1. peel

2. flit

3. flight

4. think

5. trouble

6. simplify

7. shrewd

8. children

9. catholic

10. hallucinate

11. brought

12. moody

13. wishful

14. vanity

15. rather

16. dawn

17. Donald

18. fleece

19. fleas

20. raising

21. racing

22. loan

23. long

24. judging

25. masher

26. measure

27. core

28. poor

29. cloud

30. look

31. luck

32. Luke

33. huge

34. whenever

35. therapeutic

36. able

37. ability

38. prepare

39. preparation

40. encased

41. fazed

42. judgmental

(C) Write out these sentences in phonemic transcription.

1. All of a sudden it began to rain.

2. Just thirty-four of them came to the dance.

3. I would rather have another beer.

4. Sandy suddenly turned to Connie and said, "Buckle up!"

5. Now is the time for all good men to come to the aid of their party.

6. I think that there will never be a poem lovely as a tree.

7. Not all members of the jury panel were in agreement.

8. Charlotte and Charles gave Judy some rouge for her birthday.

Forms: Morphemes and Allomorphs

In a language such as English, the changes in form that words undergo are typically associated with **endings** (and to a lesser extent with beginnings). Note, for example, all the many endings that a word like need can take:

(1) need + -s

"He needs me and I need him."

(2) need + -ed

"They needed to see us because they had long needed money."

(3) need + -ing

"They're always needing something."

(4) need + -ful

"You are a very needful child."

(5) need + -y

"We plan to give more to the poor and needy next year."

(6) need + i + ness

"I am embarrassed by his constant neediness."

(7) un- + need + -ed

"The child was surrounded by dozens of unneeded toys."

Each of the words in nos. 1–7 above is divided into its component parts by a + sign. Of all the component parts, only need can stand alone and still convey meaning, as the following will prove:

I have a great
$$\begin{cases} \text{need} \\ \text{*ed} \\ \text{*ing} \\ \text{*ful} \\ \text{*y} \\ \text{*ness} \\ \text{*un} \end{cases}$$

Thus, need as a *unit of meaning*, or **morpheme** (from the Greek morph 'form' + -eme 'unit'), is known as a **FREE MORPHEME** because it can stand alone and convey meaning independently. Morphemes such as /s/, /ed/, /ing/, /ful/, /y/ and so forth are called **BOUND MORPHEMES** because to convey meaning they must be **bound** ('attached') to a free morpheme.

There are *two types of bound morphemes:* **inflectional** and **derivational**. **Derivational** morphemes—nos. 4–7 in the list—typically change the free morpheme's part of speech when they are added; thus -ful + need (a noun) gives the adjective needful; -ness + needy (an adjective) gives the noun neediness, etc. **Inflectional** morphemes on the other hand do not change the free morpheme's part of speech; instead, they indicate *categories within that part of speech,* such as (noun) plurality, third-person subject (verb), past tense (verb), past participle (verb), or present participle (verb). Thus need as a verb can co-occur with the following **inflectional morphemes**:

need (the free morpheme as **base form**, also known as the **LV** 'lexical verb')

need + /s/ (third-person singular present tense form)

need + /ed/ (the past tense and the past participle form)

need + /ing/ (the present participle form)

/z/—Some Highly Productive English Morphemes

The several /z/ morphemes are highly productive because they involve five separate functions in English grammar, all of which occur with great frequency. Each of the /z/ morphemes has its own function. The individual /z/ morphemes have these functions:

(1) to mark **noun pluralization**: bus → buses; glove → gloves; cat → cats

(2) to mark possession (in the **genitive case**): the farmer's daughter; the book's price; the dogs' bones

(3) to mark a verb form as a **third-person singular present tense**:
  "Sue runs and I run too."
  "He knows what we know."

(4) to function as the contracted remnant of has (as in "Al's been drinking again" ['Al has been drinking again'])

(5) to function as the contracted remnant of is ("He's practically an alcoholic now") ['He is practically an alcoholic now']

Just as a phoneme can be considered an abstract representation of the way a set of sounds is actually pronounced, so a **morpheme** is an abstract representation of one or more actual forms. Those actual forms are called **allomorphs**. By examining the ways /z/ is realized, we come to understand why a morpheme whose orthographic representation is "(e)s" should be labeled /z/. Here is a description of how /z/ is realized:

RULE 1—"SCHWA ADDITION": /z/ is realized as [əz]

If the free morpheme ends in any **sibilant consonant** whether voiced or voiceless—/s z š ž č ǰ/—then you realize /z/ as [əz]. Examples:

/čṛč/ + /z/ = [čṛč-əz]
/kÍs/ + /z/ = [kÍs-əz]
/wÍš/ + /z/ = [wÍš-əz]
/bes/ + /z/ = [bés-əz]

RULE 2—"VOICING": /z/ is realized as [z]

If the free morpheme ends in any **nonsibilant voiced phoneme** (whether consonant or vowel), then you realize /z/ as [z]. Examples:

/pe/ + /z/ = [pez]
/boi/ + /z/ = [boiz]
/tʌb/ + /z/ = [tʌbz]
/gɪv/ + /z/ = [gɪvz]
/brid/ + /z/ = [bridz]
/hæŋ/ + /z/ – [hæŋz]

RULE 3—"DEVOICING": /z/ is realized as [s]

If the free morpheme ends in any **nonsibilant voiceless** phoneme (consonants only), then you realize /z/ as [s]. Examples:

/čif/ + /z/ = [čifs]
/smɪθ/ + /z/ = [smɪθs]
/hæt/ + /z/ = [hæts]

As we can see, two of the three allomorphs contain [z] (rules 1 and 2), so their abstract representation is logically /z/.

EXERCISE 1.7

(A) Provide the correct allomorph of the /z/ morpheme for each of the following base forms. (Remember: English orthography can be misleading, so it's a good idea to write out a word in phonemic transcription if you are not sure what its word-final segment actually is.)

1. catch	12. die
2. climb	13. slip
3. miss	14. feed
4. hit	15. tough
5. squash	16. evening
6. play	17. save
7. bill	18. pollute
8. date	19. try
9. fee	20. weigh
10. kick	21. gouge
11. slow	22. raise

/d/—Some Additional Highly Productive English Morphemes

The /d/ morphemes represent four very significant and frequently used functions, among them the contraction of two different verbs. The /d/ morphemes have these uses:

(1) to function as the **simple past tense** of all regular English verbs (thus: talk + -ed: "I talked with him recently.")

(2) to function as the **past participle** of all regular English verbs in exactly the same manner (thus talk + -ed: "I have talked with him frequently over the years.")

(3) to function as a contraction of had ("Joe'd better be here by 10!")

(4) to function as a contraction of would ("Joe'd be here sooner if he could")

Just as we have three allomorphs of /z/, so we also have three allomorphs of /d/. And the similarity does not end there. As /z/ becomes [əz], so does /d/ become [əd], receiving a support vowel—the schwa—under very similar circumstances; what is more, /d/ (again like /z/) has both voiced and voiceless allomorphs. Here are /d/'s morphological rules:

RULE 1—"SCHWA ADDITION": /d/ is realized as [əd]

If the free morpheme's last segment is /t/ or /d/, then morpheme /d/→ [əd]. Examples:

/het/ + /d/ = [hét-əd]
/nid/ + /d/ = [níd-əd]
/dæd/ + /d/ = [dǽd-əd] ("Dad'd already seen it")

RULE 2—"VOICING": /d/ is realized as [d]

If the free morpheme's last segment is any **voiced phoneme** *except* /d/, then morpheme /d/→[d]. Examples:

/pe/ + /d/ = [ped]
/sno/ + /d/ = [snod]
/græb/ + /d/ = [græbd]
/jʌǰ/ + /d/ = [jʌǰd]

RULE 3—"DEVOICING": /d/ is realized as [t]

If the free morpheme's last segment is any **voiceless phoneme** *except* /t/, then morpheme /d/→[t]. Examples:

/mæč/ + /d/ = [mæčt]
/kɪs/ + /d/ = [kɪst]
/ʌn-ṛθ/ + /d/ = [ʌn-ṛθt]
/kek/ + /d/ = [kekt]

Problems with /d/

Both the perception (hearing) and the production (pronouncing) of **clusters of consonants at the end of words** can cause problems for native and non-native speakers alike. This is especially true if the clusters consist of a stop or affricate consonant such as /p/, /č/, or /k/ in combination with (and typically followed by) a /t/, or such combinations as /b/, /ǰ/, or /g/ followed by /d/. In combinations like p̲t̲ (/slɛpt/), b̲d̲ (/skrʌbd/), č̲t̲ (/wačt/), ǰ̲d̲ (/ǰʌǰd/), k̲t̲ (/kɪkt/), and g̲d̲ (/rɪgd/), the /t/ and the /d̲/ tend to get "lost," i.e., not heard clearly or not pronounced perceptibly. Persons speaking English slowly and carefully will indeed pronounce the /t/ and the /d/ in these word-final consonant clusters, but in faster, less careful speech, a certain loss—whether apparent or real—may indeed occur. This is one reason why non-native speakers learning English have trouble with the second segment of these consonant clusters, which, as a simple past or past participle marker, occurs frequently and cannot always be reconstructed from context. Thus a sentence like the following

/wì-wáčt-ðə-trénz-klós-lì/

could be (mis-)interpreted as either containing a verb in the simple present—

"We watch the trains closely."

or else containing a verb in the simple past—

"We watched the trains closely."

if the /t/ is not carefully articulated and clearly heard.

EXERCISE 1.8

(A) Provide the correct allomorph of morpheme /d/ for each of the following base forms.

1. scratch

2. look

3. guild

4. scream

5. free

6. tip

7. kill

8. pay

9. nab

10. warn

11. knit

12. wash

13. arrange

14. divorce

15. fit

16. slap

17. goad

18. cough

19. agree

20. cry

21. knife

22. bid

(B) When combined with the appropriate allomorph of /d/, which of the items in exercise section (A) above might prove difficult—because of consonant clusters—to perceive or produce?

(C) What mistake in /d/ allomorph choice might be made by learners of English as a foreign/second language who paid excessive attention to spelling?

2

VERBS AND TENSES; FORMS AND FUNCTIONS

Verbs' Forms

In English, a main or lexical verb is any word that can be **conjugated**, i.e., that can add the morphemes /ing/, /d/, and /z/ to mark, respectively, present participle, past tense/past participle, and third person singular present tense.

Regular Verbs

Approximately 98% of all English verbs are **morphologically regular** ('regular as to form'). English regular verbs all have just four forms: the **base** form, the **-s** form, the **-ed** form, and the **-ing** form. The **base form** is used throughout the present tense except in 3.sg. (the third person singular); the base form also constitutes the imperative, appears as the second element in the future and the conditional tenses, and makes up the second element in modal constructions. When preceded by the preposition to, the base form constitutes the infinitive, which is widely used in complementizing clauses (see ch. 8). The morphology of the forms /z/ (3.sg. present tense) and /d/ (simple past and past participle) has already been discussed (see ch. 1, pp. 38–39 and 43–44). The /ing/ form constitutes the present participle. Examples of all the four forms of a **regular verb** (i.e., a four-form verb whose forms manifest no vowel or consonant changes whatsoever) are now presented:

process (the **base form**)
    —to process (the infinitive):
        "I want to process these applications."
    —I/You/We/They process (i.e., the 1.sg. [first person singular],
        2.sg., and 1.pl./2.pl./3.pl. present tense forms, that is to
        say, **all** present tense forms that are not 3.sg., for which see
        below)
    —process (imperative = the command form):
        "Process these applications right now!"
    —will process (future tense):
        "I will process 500,000 more applications tonight."
    —would process (conditional tense):
        "I would process even more if I could."

—might process (a modal construction [see ch. 4]):
> "I might process all the applications for the whole country."

processes (the **third-person singular present tense form**): "He processes applications for the fun of it." "That new computer processes with incredible speed." (Etc., etc. **Any** singular subject that is not first person—I—or second person—you—is automatically third person, a fact which emphasizes the third person singular's great importance. [The same is true in the plural: any person not first—we—or second—you—is automatically third.])

processed (the **past tense** form **and** the **past participle** form):
> PAST TENSE:
> "I processed vast quantities of data yesterday."
> PAST PARTICIPLE (which is typically used in **perfect tenses** [see pp. 46–47]):
> "I have processed all of three applications today."

processing (the **present participle** [which is typically used in **progressive** tenses, for which see pp. 58–62]/gerund form):
> "I was processing that data when the phone rang."
> "I enjoy word processing."

Irregular Verbs

The 300 or so English verbs that are **irregular** (which constitute only about 2% of the total number of verbs in the language but include many that are frequently used) have either three, four, five, or even eight forms.

Many irregular verbs have FIVE forms: three of the forms just presented for process (base, 3.sg. present, present participle) plus **non-identical forms for the past tense and the past participle**. An example of a five-form irregular verb is break, whose five forms are compared here with the regular verb process. (All differences between the two are highlighted in bold letters.)

> break / process (BASE)
> breaks / processes (3.SG.PRESENT)
> **broke** / processed (PAST TENSE)
> **broken** / processed (PAST PARTICIPLE)
> breaking / processing (PRESENT PARTICIPLE)

If break were regular, its past tense and past participle forms would both be *breaked. As an irregular verb, however, its past tense form is characterized by **ablauting** ('any vowel change that alternates') in which /e/ → /o/ (/brek/ → /brok/) and its past participle form is characterized by both ablauting and /(e)n/ addition. Ablauting involves many different types of vowel changes. Here are some of them:

/u/ → /ʌ/, /I/ (do → does, did)
/e/ → /ɛ/ (say → says, said)
/ɛ/ → /ɔ/ (catch → caught)
/I/ → /æ/ (sit → sat)
/ʌ/ → /æ/ (run → ran)
/I/ → /æ/, /ʌ/ (drink → drank, drunk)
/i/ → /e/ (eat → ate)
/ai/ → /u/, /o/ (fly → flew, flown)
/o/ → /ɔ/ (go → gone)

Almost without exception, and even in irregular verbs, the 3.sg.pres. form is eminently predictable as: BASE + (e)s (morpheme /z/); we thus have processes, breaks, etc. However, there are four verbs—be, do, have, and say—that **constitute exceptions to this rule**. Be is particularly exceptional as an eight-form verb—the only one in the language—with three irregular present-tense forms (as well as two irregular pasts and an irregular past participle). We will now compare be with our archetypical regular verb process. All the irregular forms of be are highlighted in bold type.

> **be** / process (BASE)
> **am** / process (1.SG.PRESENT)
> **are** / process (2.SG./PL.PRESENT, ALL PRESENT PLURALS)
> **is** / processes (3.SG.PRESENT)
> **was** / processed (1.SG./3.SG. PAST)
> **were** / processed (ALL REMAINING PAST)
> **been** / processed (PAST PARTICIPLE)
> being / processing (PRESENT PARTICIPLE)

Another verb whose 3.sg. present tense forms deviate from the norm is have:

> have / process
> **has** / processes (3.SG. PRESENT)
> **had** / processed
> having / processing

The same is true of do, whose vowel sound undergoes ablauting in the 3.sg. present. (Note that the orthography masks the irregularity, giving the false impression that the form is actually regular.)

> do [du] / process
> **does** [dʌz]/ processes (3.SG. PRESENT)
> **did** / processed
> doing / processing

Orthography also masks irregularity in the 3.sg. present of <u>say</u>:

say [se] / process
says [sɛz] / processes
said / processed
saying / processing

The remaining irregular verbs involve **irregularity only in the past and/or past participle forms**, and fit the following nine morphological patterns:

THE NINE MORPHOLOGICAL PATTERNS OF IRREGULAR VERBS

3-form:
identical base/past/past part[iciple]:
<u>bet</u>

4-form:
identical **past**/past part.:
The three subcategories' model verbs are:
<u>catch</u>   <u>sit</u>   <u>spend</u>
identical **base**/past part.:
<u>run</u>

5-form (all have **non-identical** base/past/past part.):
ablauting only:
<u>drink</u>
(e)n marking past part. plus ablauting:
<u>eat</u>   <u>break</u>   <u>fly</u>

We will now examine each of these nine patterns separately. (From here on, those forms—3.sg.pres. and pres.part.—which show no irregularity do not appear. Thus the only forms we list and comment on are: base, past, and past participle.)

THREE-FORM VERBS

Verbs like <u>bet</u> have identical base/past/past part. forms:

<u>bet</u> (base; past; past part.)

FOUR-FORM VERBS

(A) Identical past/past participle:

(1) both ablauting and consonant difference:
catch:
> catch [kɛč][1] (base)
> caught [kɔt][2] (past; past part.)

(2) ablauting only:
sit:
> sit (base)
> sat (past; past part.)

(3) consonant difference only:
spend:
> spend (base)
> spent (past; past part.)

(B) Identical base/past participle:
Ablauting only:
run:
> run (base; past part.)
> ran (past)

FIVE-FORM VERBS (all with **non-identical** base/past/past part.):

(A) Ablauting only:
drink:
> drink (base)
> drank (past)
> drunk (past part.)

(B) -(e)n marking past part. plus ablauting:

(1) two different vowel sounds:

—**same vowel in** *base* **and past part.:**
eat:
> eat (base)
> ate (past)
> eaten (past part.)

—**same vowel in** *past* **and past part.:**

break:

> break (base)
> broke (past)
> broken (past part.)

(2) **three different vowel sounds:**

fly:

> fly (base)
> flew (past)
> flown (past part.)

Two highly frequent five-form verbs—do, and go—do not conform to any of the above patterns and must be treated individually as "eccentrics." (Phonetic transcription and commentary is added.)

do:

> do [du] (base)
> did [dɪd] (past) (ablauting but /d/ regularity)
> done [dʌn] (past part.) (ablauting with -n)

go:

> go [go] (base)
> went (past) (this form is phonetically unrelatable to the verb's base)
> gone [gɔn] (past part.)

EXERCISE 2.1

(A) Give the past and the past participle forms for each of the following verbs. Then tell whether the verb is regular or irregular, and, if irregular, which of the nine irregularity verb patterns it conforms to.

1. become

2. blink

3. bring

4. call

5. cost

6. dig

7. drown

8. fall

9. have

10. hear

11. hold

12. injure

13. know

14. leave

15. lend

16. let

17. make

18. mean

19. milk

20. need

21. read

22. ride

23. ring

24. lie [two answers]

25. see

26. sell

27. send

28. shake

29. sleep

30. slide

31. spring

32. steal

33. strike

34. sweep

35. swim

36. take

37. teach

38. tear [something]

39. tell

40. think

41. transcribe	**45.** welcome
42. try	**46.** win
43. wear	**47.** write
44. weep	

(B) Tell whether each of the following forms is **base, past, past participle** or two or more of these classifications simultaneously (and, if so, which).

1. gave	**7.** rode
2. led	**8.** blew
3. smile	**9.** paid
4. given	**10.** taken
5. hid	**11.** put
6. ridden	**12.** ring

13. rang

14. thrown

15. swung

16. sought

17. cut

18. came

19. decide

20. done

21. missed

22. blown

23. stank

24. went

25. tune

26. founded

27. drove

28. got

29. bring

30. woven

Verb Tenses and Auxiliary Verbs: The Non-Modal Auxiliaries (do, be, have) and the Modal Auxiliaries

The Simple Tenses

English has only two simple tenses: present and past. The morphology of the simple tenses verb forms has already been examined, so only a quick review will be given here of a regular verb—call—in conjugation:

THE REGULAR VERB call IN CONJUGATION: THE TWO SIMPLE TENSES

PRESENT:

person (= subject)	**singular**	**plural**
1st (the person speaking)	I call	we call
2nd (person being spoken to)	you call	you call
3rd (person or thing spoken about)	he	
	she } calls	they call
	it	

PAST:

		singular	**plural**
1st		I called	we called
2nd		you called	you called
3rd		he	
		she } called	they called
		it	

The Importance of the Subject

As can be seen by the repetitiousness of the above chart—just three different words (calls, call, and called) in a total of 12 separate slots or positions—, conjugations are mainly irrelevant exercises in a language like English where the vast majority of verbs—including many irregular verbs—have four forms only. It is this very repetitiousness of form that makes English so reluctant to drop its subject pronouns. A sentence such as the following is ungrammatical for precisely that reason:

*Anyway, told me to pay but said that couldn't.

The grammatical version of this sentence would have to read something like this:

Anyway, he told me to pay but I said that I couldn't.

With few exceptions, all verbs in English require a subject to appear in the **surface structure**, i.e., in the sentence's final product (as opposed to its **deep structure** or underlying representation). Without an overt subject, most English verb forms do not tell us who is doing the action or assuming the state.

Imperatives ('Direct Command Forms'), the Present Tense, and the Excluded Subject Pronoun

Only present tense forms can be used in **imperatives** because one can only command someone to do something "now" (at the present moment), not "then" (at some past moment). (Thus "Stop doing that!" but never *"Stopped doing that!") Likewise, only second person pronouns can serve as the (implied) subject of an imperative construction, since a direct command can only be made of someone we are speaking to, not about. Direct commands often exclude their implied (or underlying) subject pronoun you—

> Come inside right now!
> Play nicely with the other children.
> Please sit here.

but can reinstate the you at will, often to make the command more emphatic or forceful, thus:

> You come inside right now!
> You play nicely with the other children, you hear?!

The Compound Tenses: Present and Past

A **compound tense** is one in which each (pro)noun's corresponding verb consists of two or more words. (Thus have called or have been calling are compound, whereas call is not a compound but a **simple tense**.) There are two main types of present or past compound tenses: **perfect**, and **progressive**. A third type—**perfect progressive**—combines the two. (Note that only the active voice is being treated in this chapter. The passive-voice tenses will be dealt with in ch. 4. All passives are compounds.)

Present perfect and **past perfect** tenses consist of two elements: a conjugated form of the non-modal auxiliary verb have plus the **past participle** of the **lexical verb (LV)** in question. (The lexical or "main" verb is always the primary content-bearing part of any perfect-tense form.) Since have is conjugated, it is marked for person, number, and tense, whereas the past participle—never conjugated—is never marked for person/number/tense. Thus have changes form whereas the past participle does not.

What follow are several examples of the **present perfect** and the **past perfect** tenses:

PRESENT PERFECT:

We have eaten enough.

pres.	past
tense	part.
of	of the
non-	LV
modal	eat
aux.	
have	

She has talked to him before.
They have been very busy.

PAST PERFECT:

We had eaten enough.

past	past
tense	part.
of	of the
non-	LV
modal	eat
aux.	
have	

She had talked to him before.
They had been very busy.

Present progressive and **past progressive** tenses also consist of two elements: a conjugated form of the non-modal auxiliary verb be, plus the (never-conjugated) present participle of the particular LV. Here are some examples:

PRESENT PROGRESSIVE:

We are just killing time.

pres.	present
tense	part.
of	of
non-	LV
modal	kill
aux.	
be	

You are being very bad.

PAST PROGRESSIVE:

I was just killing time.

past	present
tense	part.
of	of
non-	LV
modal	kill
aux.	
be	

You were being very bad.

Compound tenses consisting of **three** elements are the **present perfect progressive** and the **past perfect progressive**. The three elements are these:

—a conjugated form of the non-modal aux. have
—been (the past participle of be)
—the present participle of the particular LV

Here are some examples of these two perfect progressive tenses:

PRESENT PERFECT PROGRESSIVE:

We have been eating too much.

pres.	past	pres.
tense	part.	part.
of	of	of
have	be	LV eat

PAST PERFECT PROGRESSIVE:

We had been eating too much.

past	past	pres.
tense	part.	part.
of	of	of
have	be	LV eat

The Compound Tenses: Future and Conditional

It is important to be aware that the English tenses normally labeled "future" and "conditional" **are themselves compounds**, not simple tenses as are their equivalents in languages such as Spanish and other Romance languages. The English **future tense** consists of the modal auxiliary will plus the particular LV's base form; thus:

> *FUTURE TENSE:*
>   She will speak to them about it soon.
>   modal   base
>   aux.   form of
>   will   the LV speak

The construction that we label (for the sake of convenience) the English **conditional tense** consists of the **modal auxiliary would** plus the particular LV's base form; thus:

> *CONDITIONAL TENSE:*
>   If she wanted to, she would speak to them about it soon.
>   modal   base
>   aux.   form of
>   would   the LV speak

This conditional **form**, or construction (the modal auxiliary would plus the particular LV's base form) has at least three functions: (1) true conditionality, (2) "future-in-the-past," and (3) habitual action (or state) in the past. The **true conditionality** function is treated extensively at the end of ch. 4 (pp. 151–54) and can be illustrated here by the following sentence:

> If I had any money I would buy a new car.

The **"future-in-the-past"** function of the conditional form is exemplified by a sentence such as this—

> He said he would leave at midnight.—

which is simply a past-tense version of:

> He says he will leave at midnight.

And the **"habitual action in the past"** function is illustrated thus:

> Back then, he would arrive at 10 and stay all day.

The future and conditional constructions with <u>will</u> and <u>would</u>, respectively, are often referred to as **synthetic future tense** and **synthetic conditional tense**, terms which explicitly contrast these two tenses with the **periphrastic future tense** and the **periphrastic conditional tense**. In the periphrastic constructions, use is made of the semi-auxiliary peri-modal phrase <u>BE going to</u> (in which <u>BE</u> is the conjugated element) to express certain types of futurity or conditionality. Here are some examples of the periphrastic future and the periphrastic "conditional":[3]

<table>
<tr><td><u>PERIPHRASTIC FUTURE:</u></td><td><u>PERIPHRASTIC "CONDITIONAL":</u></td></tr>
<tr><td>I am <u>going to</u> leave soon.</td><td>I <u>was going to</u> leave soon.</td></tr>
<tr><td>They <u>are going to</u> pass.</td><td>They <u>were going to</u> pass.</td></tr>
</table>

While the two periphrastic tenses are said to convey the impression of imminence and certainty (that something is just about to happen), the synthetic tenses supposedly imply a somewhat more remote prediction. At times, however, the difference between the impressions that each set conveys is largely stylistic, with the periphrastic tenses preferred in informal/colloquial speech and the synthetic tenses in more formal language.

Both the synthetic future-marking modal <u>will</u> along with the synthetic conditional-marking modal <u>would</u> combine with forms of the non-modal auxiliaries <u>have</u> and <u>be</u> to produce future or conditional perfect, future or conditional progressive, and future or conditional perfect progressive tenses for a total of six additional compound tenses. Here are some examples of these six additional tenses:

THE FUTURES:
    future perfect:
        She <u>will have spoken</u> to him by this time tomorrow.
    future progressive:
        She <u>will be speaking</u> to him soon.
    future perfect progressive:
        She <u>will have been speaking</u> to him for an hour by this time
            tomorrow.

THE CONDITIONALS:
    conditional perfect:
        She <u>would have spoken</u> to him if she could.
    conditional progressive:
        She <u>would be speaking</u> to him now if he were here.
    conditional perfect progressive:
        She <u>would have been speaking</u> to me now if I had let her.

When we add these six tenses to the eight that we examined earlier in this chapter, we come up with a total of **fourteen active-voice compound tenses** in English. The following chart displays all 14 tenses. (The chart includes parenthetical space for the only two tenses—the present and the past—that are not compound but **simple,** as we already know.)

THE FOURTEEN ACTIVE-VOICE COMPOUND (AND THE TWO ACTIVE-VOICE SIMPLE) TENSES

		PERFECTS	PROGRESSIVES	PERF. PROGS.
futures:	fut.	fut. perf.	fut. prog.	fut. perf. prog.
conditionals:	cond.	cond. perf.	cond. prog.	cond. perf. prog.
presents:	**(simple present)**	pres. perf.	pres. prog.	pres. perf. prog.
pasts:	**(simple past)**	past perf.	past prog.	past perf. prog.

EXERCISE 2.2

(A) Underline each of the simple or compound verb tenses appearing below, then identify each one as to tense. Note that some of the verb forms will appear as infinitives, i.e., without tense (tenseless).

1. I have told you what I think about him.

2. We will obey your orders.

3. What has become of Baby Jane?

4. Many have called but few have answered.

5. I had been searching for them since Monday.

6. In all likelihood they will have left by now.

7. I just get so upset; I just don't know.

8. All my friends were there and gave me presents.

9. They are refusing to cross the picket line.

10. They wouldn't have been staying at grandma's house because she went to the cabin to prepare for the weekend.

11. You said you'd be coming in on the six o'clock flight.

12. He is taller than I was at that age.

13. I would have written you if I had found the time.

14. They know what I did.

15. He went out and got some bread.

16. By the year 2002, Vince will have been teaching for 30 years.

17. She's going to buy me a peanut butter and jelly sandwich.

18. She said she would meet me on the terrace at noon.

19. I have been looking for you all my life.

20. They were going to tell us they had already disposed of the body.

(B) Write a sentence containing a verb form that corresponds to each of these descriptions. Use any LV, person, and number.

    1. present

    2. past progressive

    3. synthetic future

    4. periphrastic future

    5. synthetic conditional

    6. periphrastic conditional

    7. future perfect

    8. past perfect

    9. future perfect progressive

    10. past

11. present perfect

12. present progressive

13. conditional perfect

14. conditional progressive

15. future progressive

Verb Tense Meanings and Uses

The following sections provide information about how the various tense **forms** are used in differing **functions** to convey meaning, and what different sorts of meaning they each convey. Throughout our discussion we will contrast **tense** (the marked-for-tense verb forms themselves) with **time** (which among other things refers to time on a chronological scale: the present moment, the future-yet-to-come, the immediate past, the more remote past, and so forth).

The Present Tense

An overworked tense in English, "the present" can have reference to **present time**, to **future time**, and even in a limited way to **past time**.

In a **present time usage**, the present tense conveys these meanings:

(a) reference to the **actual present moment**, i.e., to what is happening at this very moment—a function which is actually more typical of the present progressive tense (for which see below) than of the present tense. This "present-moment" reference often involves someone's describing what someone else is doing right now, as in, for example, an opera broadcast:

> Maddalena falls into the arms of don Vincenzo and swears eternal love even as he plunges the dagger deep into her treacherous heart while she breathes her dying breath. She now expires, and Vincenzo begins to sob uncontrollably as the curtain falls on the final act of Massimo Verismo's "La Forza Delle Putane."

(b) reference to what is performed and accomplished just by virtue of its being said—the so-called **performative** verb. Examples:

> I now pronounce you man and wife.
>> [By virtue of pronouncing the words "man and wife," the couple are now, indeed, married.]
> We condemn you to 99 years at hard labor.
> The judge sentenced him to life in prison.
> The priest blessed their union.
> I now declare you husband and wife.

(c) reference to a longer, ongoing stretch of time involving a **stative** verb, one which refers to states of being or states of possessing (as opposed to actions). Examples:

> I have five income properties on the north side of Chicago.
> She knows the names and capitals of all the world's 198 countries.

(d) reference to a longer, ongoing stretch of time involving a **durative** verb, one whose action—repeated or habitual—is even less closely tied to the present moment than is a stative's. Examples:

By day he gambles and by night he drinks and carries on.
You, on the other hand, work too much and study too hard.

(e) reference to a fraternal twin of both statives and duratives known as the **timeless truth**:

Greenland is near the North Pole.
The Andes Mountains run the length of the South American continent.
Three constitutes the square root of nine.

In a **future time usage**, the present tense is employed for two purposes:

(a) to refer to events which are **scheduled or planned on**, e.g.,

The hunger strike begins tomorrow at dawn.
The ship sets sail at 1 p.m. on Friday, Nov. 13th.

Note that if the event is **not** scheduled or planned, the present tense will **not** serve to express future time usage and the synthetic or periphrastic future must be used instead. Example:

*Do you promise you bring me back something from Hawaii, Daddy?
→ → → Do you promise you will bring me back something . . .
or: Do you promise you are going to bring me back . . .

(b) to refer to an unscheduled future event in a subordinate clause of a sentence **whose main clause is in the future tense**:

I'll pay you back when the check arrives.
main clause   subordinate clause

She will turn you into the cops as soon as she has
m a i n   c l a u s e   subordinate clause

some hard evidence of your nefarious doings.
(subordinate clause [continued])

In a **past time usage**, the present tense's only function—and it is a very limited one—is to narrate the so-called "historical present" whereby the past is made more immediate and vivid when it is brought forward into the present. Example:

I once murdered someone. It was a dark and stormy night. I was walking down Broadway when all of a sudden this drunken bum falls out of a doorway, staggers, sticks his hand in his mouth and starts to vomit all over the place. So I go up to him and I say, " . . . "

The Past Tense

There are three uses to which the English past tense is put in a truly past-time frame. They include

(a) a single past event:
> Joe's grandfather voted for FDR for the first time in 1936.
> Peggy Sue had a baby last night.

(b) an enduring past situation ("delineated time in the past")
> Jim worked at the envelope company for 53 years.
> Dracula was count of Transylvania from 1243–1291.

(c) repeated/habitual events in the past:
> Every morning I drove down Mesa Street to my job.
> Joe went to only twelve conferences a year until he retired.

In addition, the past tense forms are used in English to express **contrary-to-fact** or **hypothetical** statements which have no pastness about them whatsoever:

> If you were black [which you're not, but let's suppose for the sake of argument], you'd have a hard time living in certain neighborhoods.

Past tense forms are also used to express **heightened politeness** or deference when making a request:

> Sir, may I be so bold as to say that I wanted to ask for your daughter's hand in marriage.

The Future and the Conditional Tenses
FUTURE TENSE

Future time reference is the most typical function of the synthetic future tense:

> I will arrive from Dallas on the 12:05 flight.
> She will be tickled pink by this present.

In addition (and as a logical extension of the concept of future time reference), the synthetic future can express **predictions**:

> She will see to it that you never work here again.
> The Guthrie Center Cornhuskers will become a major league baseball team in four years.

CONDITIONAL TENSE

The synthetic **conditional tense forms** encompass three diametrically opposed **functions**:

(a) the traditional referents of **conditionality**—the **hypothetical** ('what we propose as possibly coming true'), the **contrary to fact**, the **unreal**, etc.:

> I would go to the movies if I didn't have to finish this job. [But I do have to finish it so I can't go, so "going to the movies" is not real and not factual.]
>
> You would tell me where to get off if I weren't your boss, wouldn't you?

(b) **repeated, habitual, recurring actions/events/states in the past:**

> I would go to the movies three times a week when I was a kid.
>
> Back then, every time you got angry at me you would tell me where to get off, wouldn't you?

Conditional form (b)'s function is so totally different from what we observe to be conditional form (a)'s function that function (b) cries out for a completely separate tense of its own. And indeed, type (b) sentences often employ the periphrastic used to as a substitute for would:

> I used to go to the movies three times a week when I was a kid.

(c) the **"future-in-the-past"** function, in which would serves as the past tense of the modal form will:

FUTURE[expressed by the **future** tense]-IN-THE-**PRESENT**:

> They say that they will wash the dog.

PRESENT	FUTURE
tense	tense
verb form	verb form

FUTURE[expressed by the **conditional** tense]-IN-THE-**PAST**:

> They said that they would wash the dog.

PAST	CONDITIONAL
tense	tense
verb form	verb form

The Progressive Tenses: Present/Past/Future/Conditional

These events or situations constitute the progressive tenses' time and aspect usages:

—**in progress**
> No doubt by this time tomorrow Nick will be arguing about something with his girlfriend.

—**repeated over time**
> They were always fighting over who should do what and to whom.

—**scheduled or planned for the future**
> So you're leaving on the midnight train to Georgia?

The Perfect Tenses: Present/Past/Future/Conditional

Perfect tenses typically span the time between "then" (when the event took place or the state was entered into) and "now" (the moment when the event/state is or was being talked about). Perfect time frames refer to **situations which have endured** from point X in the past up to right now; to past events which continue **affecting the present moment**; and to events so recent that though technically past they are still **impacting on the present**. Examples follow:

—**enduring situations:**
> Aragon and Catalonia have formed part of a united Spain since 1469.
> Austin has been the capital of Texas since 1838.

—**past events affecting the present moment:**
> I have broken my hip and cannot get around very well.
> She had been treasurer of the company for so long that she felt she owned it.

—**events so recent that they impact on the present:**
> The Hartzemanian army has just invaded Central Sorbovia!

(A) Underline each verb form. Write the name of its tense. Then write the function that the verb form is expressing.

1. [From an announcer at a basketball game:]   Treetop drives for the board, leaps, shoots, and . . . it is in!

2. [From a general at a staff meeting:]   The invasion begins at 12:01 tomorrow morning.

3. [From a jealous girlfriend:]   I will kill anyone who lays a hand on you.

4. [From an office worker reporting on his life as a commuter:]   We would always get caught in the rush hour traffic until we finally switched over to the subway.

5. [From the mouths of well-meaning friends:]   We would do anything for you—anything!—if only we had the money.

6. [From a hospital worker:]   Right now you are trying to learn what has happened to you.

7. [From the Sunday sermon:]   She had never taken a drink until that fateful night.

8. [From his best friend:]   He's getting married this Saturday.

9. [In the divorce lawyer's chambers:]   I have tried to be a good father.

10. [From the mouth of a stern parent:]   I order you to leave.

11. [The swimming coach:]   He swims 50 laps every day.

12. You were born on September 30, 1988.

13. The judge declared a mistrial.

14. [From the weekly broadcast of the Metropolitan Opera:]   As the curtain rises on Act Two, Mamma Lucia enters the square.

15. [From Mamma Lucia's doctor:]   I have no idea how she stays so healthy.

16. They said goodbye to everyone and then finally left the party.

(B) Write an original sentence illustrating each of these descriptions.

1. synthetic future tense, future time reference

2. present progressive tense, action scheduled for the future

3. present tense, present time, stative-type verb

4. present tense, past time, historical present

5. present perfect tense, very recent events impacting on the present

6. present tense, present time, timeless truth

7. present tense, present time, actual present moment

8. future progressive tense, action in progress

9. present tense, future time, scheduled/planned-on event

10. synthetic conditional tense, hypotheticality

11. present perfect tense, past events affecting present moment

12. past tense, single past event

13. synthetic conditional tense, unreality

14. past progressive tense, action repeated over time

15. present tense, future time, unscheduled event in a subordinate clause

16. present tense, present time, performative-type verb

17. past perfect, enduring situation

18. past tense, enduring past situation

19. present tense, present time, durative-type verb

20. past tense, repeated events in the past

21. synthetic future tense, prediction

22. synthetic conditional, repeated/habitual action in the past

BASIC STRUCTURES, QUESTIONS, *DO* INSERTION, NEGATION, AUXILIARIES, RESPONSES, EMPHASIS, CONTRACTION

The Five Basic Structures

Noncomplex sentences in English have five basic structures: affirmative statements, negative statements, yes/no affirmative questions, yes/no negative questions, and content questions. Here are the symbols used to represent each structure, together with an example of each one:

+ (affirmative statement):	You live here.
− (negative statement):	You don't live here./
	You do not live here.
yn + (yes/no affirmative question):	Do you live here?
yn − (yes/no negative question):	Don't you live here?/
	Do you not live here?
wh/co (wh[-word] content question):	Where do you live?
	Why do you live here?
	When do you live here? (etc.)

Two Different Types of Questions

The difference between "yes/no" questions on the one hand and "wh/content" questions on the other hand is this: *wh*/**content questions <u>can never be answered "yes" or "no"</u>**, while yes/no questions can be answered "yes" or "no" and usually are. Thus:

"Where do you live?"—*"Yes." [Quite ungrammatical.]
"Where do you live?"—"On Sixth Avenue." [Grammatical, and one of many possible answers.]

Do-Insertion

It is important to pay close attention to the presence or absence in a particular structure of the non-modal auxiliary do. Adding do to a structure is known in linguistics as *do*-**insertion**. *Do* appears exactly where we would expect it or any other verb to appear in negative statements: **right after the subject**, according to the phrase structure rules we examined in ch. 1, thus:

$S \rightarrow$ NP VP

$S \rightarrow$ You	do	not	live here.
(pro)N	aux	neg	V
NP		VP	

But this is not the case in the three interrogative structures (yn +, yn −, wh/co), where *do* appears **before the subject**:

Do	you	live	here?
aux	(pro)N	V	

When <u>do</u> appears before its subject, that is known as **auxiliary inversion**. We must always assume that the **+** statement serves as the point of departure for the other four structures. Thus the process by which we get from **+** (where we start) to **yn +** (where we want to end up) looks like this:

	1. [the + statement]	You live here.
→→→→	2. [do-insertion]	you do live here
→→→→	3. [auxiliary inversion]	do you live here
→→→→	4. [adding intonation/punctuation:]	
		Do you live here?

Negation

We should also pay close attention to the negating element <u>not</u> and how it functions syntactically. <u>Not</u> is inserted only in − and **yn -** or in a **wh/co** that is negative. The negative element <u>not</u> **always appears right after the auxiliary**. This important trait distinguishes English from most other languages, where the negating element is placed elsewhere. Here is the process by which we get from **+** to **−:**

	1. [the + statement]	You live here.
→→→→	2. [do insertion]	you do live here
→→→→	3. [not insertion]	You do not live here.

In only one type of sentence—the **yn −** structure in which <u>not</u> is **uncontracted**—does the negating element appear somewhere other than right after the auxiliary. Thus compare:

yn − contracted:	Don't you live here?
yn − uncontracted:	Do you <u>not</u> live here?

The Role of the First Auxiliary

We already know that the − , yn + , yn − and wh/co structures contain one thing that the + structure doesn't: the non-modal auxiliary <u>do</u>. If the + structure lacks an auxiliary verb (as for example "You live <u>here</u>"), you have to insert do into the negatives and the questions that come from it (thus "You don't live here," "Do you live here?", "Don't you live here?", "Where do you live?"). English auxiliary verbs are either non-modals (be/do/have) or they are modals (can/could/may/might/must/shall/should/will/would) or else peri-modals (ought to/be 3 to, etc. [see ch. 4]). English does not allow such syntactical patterns as *"You not live here", *"Not you live here?", etc. Do insertion in negatives and questions is necessary when the + statement contains no auxiliary.

Here are some examples of this in practice. All of the + structures in these examples contain auxiliaries—either non-modal be, non-modal have, or the modal auxiliary can. Therefore, do is not inserted.

	non-modal auxiliaries		**modal auxililary**
	BE as the aux	have as the aux	can as the aux
+	You are trying.	You have tried.	You can try.
−	You aren't trying.	You haven't tried.	You can't try.
yn+	Are you trying?	Have you tried?	Can you try?
yn−	Aren't you trying?	Haven't you tried?	Can't you try?
	Are you not trying?	Have you not tried?	Can you not try?
wh/co	Why are you trying?	What have you tried?	When can you try?

What we notice about these − , yn + , yn − and wh/co structures is that **none contains any form of do.** So as we already know, do **is not added to negatives and questions if the corresponding + structure already contains an auxiliary verb**.

The auxiliary plays an extremely important role in any English structure it appears in. The first auxiliary in a sentence indicates and marks **person and number** as well as **tense**. Perhaps it is no accident that the three non-modal auxiliaries do, be and have are morphologically irregular and quite varied in form. But note that while the three **non**-modal auxiliaries are varied in form, the nine **modal** auxiliaries—can, could, may, might, must, shall, should, will, and would—are **invariant**, never inflecting for person or number and lacking not only tense but present and past participles as well. (See ch. 4 for more information on modals.)

When Non-modal Auxiliaries be/do/have Are Used as Main Verbs

While be/do/have usually function as auxiliaries, they can also function in a non-auxiliary capacity as the main verb in the sentence. Here are some examples of this:

BE: I am the best cook.
DO: I do the dishes every night.
HAVE: I have many chores.

When be functions as a main verb it never allows *do*-insertion:

+	I am the best cook.	
−	I am not the best cook.	(*I do not be the best cook.)
yn+	Am I the best cook?	(*Do I be the best cook?)
yn−	Am I not the best cook?	(*Do I not be the best cook?)
wh/co	Why am I the best cook?	(*Why do I not be the best cook?)

However, **do and have both require *do*-insertion when functioning as an LV main verb:**[4]

DO:

+	I do the dishes every night.
−	I don't do the dishes every night.
yn+	Do I do the dishes every night?
yn−	Don't I do the dishes every night?
wh/co	Why do I do the dishes every night?

HAVE:

+	I have many chores.
−	I don't have many chores.
yn+	Do I have many chores?
yn−	Don't I have many chores?
wh/co	Why do I have many chores?

The *wh*-Fronting Rule

A *wh*-**word** such as who/which/what/where/when/why/whose/how can function either as the subject in its wh/co question or the object in it. Consider the following:

1. Who did he call?
2. Who called him?

In (1), the subject of the sentence is he. This can be proven:

+	He called someone.	he = subject
−	He didn't call {someone}.	called = verb
yn+	Did he call someone?	someone = object [pronoun]
yn−	Didn't he call someone?	
wh/co	Who(m) did he call?	

Sentence #2 starts out its life as + and undergoes these changes:

he called {someone}
he called {who(m)}   **substitution of wh word**
he did call {who(m)}   **do-insertion**
did he call who(m)   **auxiliary inversion**
who(m) did he call   *wh*-**fronting** (moving wh word to the front of the sentence)

This last transformation is known as the *wh*-**fronting rule** because the wh word is moved to the front of the sentence, which is then ready for the requisite intonation and punctuation to be added:

Who(m) did he call?

However, **the *wh*-fronting rule only affects *wh*-words which are objects,** not subjects. In sentence #2 (above), the wh word is a subject, so it does not get fronted. In actual fact, 2's wh word's antecedent in the + sentence was already "front" to begin with, as the following will show:

+   Someone called him.
−   Someone didn't call him.
yn+   Did someone call him?
yn   Didn't someone call him?
wh/co Who called him?

Here, who merely substitutes for the indefinite pronoun someone which already serves as the subject throughout the other four basic structures. So **since someone already appears at front, no fronting rule can apply.**

EXERCISE 3.1

(A) Fill in the blanks with the corresponding absent structures. Be sure to retain the same tense throughout each set. There are usually several ways to fill in the wh/co blank since there are eight *wh*-words and almost as many wh/co questions for them to function in.

1. + We know them.

  − _____.

  yn+ _____.

  yn− _____.

  wh/co _____.

2. + _____.

  − _____.

  yn+ _____.

  yn− Don't they pay their bills?

  wh/co _____.

3. + _____.

  − I don't understand that.

  yn+ _____.

  yn− _____.

  wh/co _____.

4. + _____.

  − _____.

  yn+ Did I speak to you?

  yn− _____.

  wh/co _____.

5. + _____.

  − _____.

  yn+ _____.

  yn− _____.

  wh/co When do you arrive?

6. \+   _____.

     −   She isn't practicing enough.

     yn+   _____.

     yn−   _____.

     wh/co _____.

7. \+   He has been sick.

     −   _____.

     yn+   _____.

     yn−   _____.

     wh/co _____.

8. \+   _____.

     −   _____.

     yn+   _____.

     yn−   Wouldn't he know when to go?

     wh/co _____.

9. \+   _____.

     −   I won't tell you his name.

     yn+   _____.

     yn−   _____.

     wh/co _____.

10. \+   _____.

     −   _____.

     yn+   _____.

     yn−   _____.

     wh/co Whom had he been talking to?

11. \+   _____.

     −   _____.

     yn+   Has it turned out nicely?

     yn−   _____.

     wh/co _____.

(B) Provide one example of each of these products or processes at work.

    1. *do*-insertion

    2. the *wh*-fronting rule

    3. auxiliary inversion

    4. be as a non-modal auxiliary

    5. do as an LV

    6. a *wh*-word as object

    7. a *wh*- word as subject

    8. a wh/co question

(C) Write statements or questions corresponding to the following descriptions.

    1. yn+ ; know as LV

    2. wh/co; stay as LV; wh word as subject

3. − ; <u>own</u> as LV

4. + ; <u>write</u> as LV

5. yn−; <u>kill</u> as LV

6. wh/co; <u>leave</u> as LV; <u>wh</u> word as object

7. wh/co; <u>drop</u> as LV; <u>wh</u> word as subject

8. yn+ ; <u>tell</u> as LV

Selection Questions

A **selection question** combines two or more yn+ questions into a single inter-rogative event. The coordinating conjunction o̲r̲ typically serves as the tie-in element. Thus:

yn+ # 1:   Do you want to fly to New York?
yn+ # 2:   Do you want to drive to Miami?
combined: Do you want to fly to New York or drive to Miami?

This selection question—combined nos. 1 and 2—can no longer be answered "yes" or "no" the way its two component parts could. Instead, you have to select one of the several choices offered:

Q: "Do you want to fly to New York or drive to Miami?"

Possible answers:

1. I want to fly to New York.
2. Fly.
3. New York.
4. The former.
5. Whatever you say.
   (etc.)

Declarative Questions

A **declarative question** is a yes/no question (either + or –) which lacks aux-iliary inversion, *do*-insertion, etc.; therefore, declarative questions **manifest the same word order as declarative structures** (the + sentence). Compare:

+   You want a sandwich.
yn+   Do you want a sandwich? [do insertion, aux invers]
declarative   You want a sandwich? [said with rising intonation]
   question

Declarative questions are very similar to echo questions (see immediately below) in that they are either used to express shock or surprise or else to solicit simple verification. In colloquial and informal English, declarative questions are frequent, as are **yn+ and yn– questions which lack the auxiliary verb**, as in the following examples:

Do you want to go now? → You want to go now?
Don't you have any money? → You have any money?
Are you ready to leave? → You ready to leave?
Is he studying already? → He studying already?

Echo Questions

Echo questions are "recapitulatory" in that they repeat, directly or in paraphrase, all or part of what someone else has just said, either to confirm it or to express surprise or disbelief. An echo question typically employs rising intonation. Examples:

1. "Yesterday I bought a BMW."—"You bought a **BMW**?"
2. "I want some slivovitz."—"You want some **what**?"
3. "The two-bedroom bungalow in Beverly Hills costs only $2,000,000."—"It costs **how much**?"

Echo questions can also function as "questions about questions" in which the listener speculates on or makes fun of a question someone else just asked. Often the question about a question is so obvious as to be amusing:

4. "Is Bill Gates a billionaire?"—"Is Bill Gates a billionaire? Is the pope Catholic?"

Tag Questions

A **tag question** always appears—following a comma in writing—as **the sole interrogative element in what is otherwise a non-interrogative sentence.** A tag question's purpose is to get the listener to confirm or deny what the speaker has just stated in the (non-interrogative) "statement" part of the sentence. There are four types of statement/tag question combinations. Two of the types contain **positive statement verbs** and thus have positive assumptions, while the other two types contain **negative statement verbs** and thus have negative assumptions. If the tag question is spoken with a **rising intonation**, then the speaker is actually in doubt as to how the question will be answered. But if the tag question is spoken with a **falling intonation**, the speaker fully expects that the question will elicit a confirmative response in which the respondent will agree with the speaker's statement. In the two charts below we (1) outline the four types of tag questions in schematic form, and then (2) exemplify and explicate each.

TAG QUESTIONS: THE FOUR TYPES IN OUTLINE FORM

(1) **POSITIVE** ASSUMPTION, **IN-DOUBT** EXPECTATION
(2) **POSITIVE** ASSUMPTION, **CONFIRMATIVE** EXPECTATION
(3) **NEGATIVE** ASSUMPTION, **IN-DOUBT** EXPECTATION
(4) **NEGATIVE** ASSUMPTION, **CONFIRMATIVE** EXPECTATION

TAG QUESTIONS: THE FOUR TYPES EXEMPLIFIED
AND EXPLAINED

(1) **positive assumption, in-doubt expectation**

He likes his boss, doesn't he? [rising intonation]

(Here the speaker is in doubt so the tag assumes nothing; the subject may or may not like his boss; we simply want to know.)

(2) **positive assumption, confirmative expectation**

He likes his boss, doesn't he? [falling intonation]

(Here the speaker assumes that the subject likes his boss; thus the speaker's tag is merely seeking to get the listener to confirm the speaker's assumption.)

(3) **negative assumption, in-doubt expectation**

He doesn't like his boss, does he? [rising intonation]

(The speaker is in doubt so the tag assumes nothing; the speaker may or may not like his boss, we simply want to know.)

(4) **negative assumption, confirmative expectation**

He doesn't like his boss, does he? [falling intonation]

(The speaker assumes the subject doesn't like his boss; thus the speaker's tag merely seeks to get the listener to confirm the speaker's assumption.)

Note that as far as the mechanics of the tag are concerned, **a negative statement always generates a positive tag, and vice versa**:

He likes . . . , doesn't he?   +   ,   −
He doesn't like . . . , does he?   −   ,   +

This is an important characteristic of tagging. But there's a fifth, though less frequent, type of statement/tag combination which involves a rising-intonation tag that typically expresses irony or sarcasm, in which both the statement and the tag are positive:

(5) "You've done your homework, have you?" [We assume he hasn't!]

Invariant Tags

An invariant tag is one whose form—negative or affirmative—is not dependent on the form the statement takes. Most invariant tags lack verb forms altogether. Examples:

> You're going to get angry again, <u>right</u>?
> They've really gone off the deep end, <u>huh</u>?
> She's getting ready to go now, <u>eh</u>?

Elliptical Responses

An **elliptical response** is a response to a yes/no question in which only part of that question is repeated in the response. Here are some examples (which give the omitted words in brackets):

(1) "Was he sick yesterday?"—"Yes, he was [sick yesterday]."
(2) "Had he been seeing a doctor regularly?"—
    "Yes, he had [been seeing a doctor regularly]."

The typical elliptical response repeats only the first verb form of the question, changing its verb form if necessary but not its tense.

EXERCISE 3.2

(A) Identify the underlined elements as (a) selection questions, (b) declarative questions, (c) echo questions, (d) tag questions, (e) invariant tags, or (f) regular [yn+, yn–, wh/co] questions.

1. <u>Would I lie to you?</u>

2. She sells seashells, <u>doesn't she?</u>

3. Ya know, our muddahs was right, <u>huh</u>, Charlie?

4. "The hamster ate the cobra."————<u>"The hamster ate the cobra?"</u>

5. "Just give me a break, man."—"You, <u>a break?"</u>

6. <u>When exactly did the perpetrator perpetrate the crime, ma'am?</u>

7. <u>Doesn't it feel good to be drawn and quartered?</u>

8. Sure and 'tis a great day for the Irish, <u>isn't it?</u>

9. <u>Do you want peanut butter or jelly?</u>

10. <u>You're going to give a million dollars to charity?</u>

11. When ya gotta go ya gotta go, <u>right?</u>

12. <u>Why's he always making the same mistake?</u>

13. <u>Why he's always making the same mistake?</u>

14. <u>They're sick? OUR children are SICK?</u>

15. They don't know what they're doing, <u>do they?</u>

(B) Give all possible tag questions for the following statements. Choose the intonation you consider most appropriate, mark it with arrows, then tell which of the five tag types your question belongs to. (In some cases there is more than one possibility.)

1. We all know what <u>his</u> story is, _____?

2. Only some of my friends came to the wedding, _____?

3. You just don't understand the issue, _____?

4. Now is the time for all good women to come to the aid of their party, _____?

5. So you've wrecked the car again, _____?

6. I get totally wasted at parties, _____?

(C) Give elliptical responses to the following questions.

1. Have you been a good little girl?—_____.

2. Will they have been working for 48 hours straight by then?
—_____.

3. But do you think he's worth $4.36 an hour?—_____.

4. Won't he tell me where to get off?—_____.

Emphasis and Emphatic Structures

English achieves emphasis in a variety of ways. One way is by **vocally stressing the word to be emphasized.** Vocal stress can involve **increased loudness, higher or lower pitch, lengthening the syllable,** or any combination thereof. Almost any word can be so emphasized. The purpose of emphasis is to shift or specify the focus of the utterance. For example, in a sentence such as:

Josie told me that you were sick.

additional stress on Josie conveys the information that it was Josie (and not someone else) who told me; additional stress on told says that the means by which the information was conveyed was verbal, not written (or that she indeed told me, despite any assertion to the contrary); stress on me emphasizes that it was not someone else whom Josie told; etc.

Another way by which English achieves emphasis is through *do insertion*, that is, by adding the appropriate tense/number form of the non-modal auxiliary verb do to the emphatic structure and then stressing that form, thereby emphasizing the action of the verb. Here is an example:

UNEMPHATIC [a plain statement of fact]:
1. Janice studies calculus every night.

EMPHATIC [possibly intended to contradict someone's assertion to the contrary]:
2. Janice does study calculus every night.

In sentence #2, does—the product of do insertion—can be viewed as a **dummy verb** in that it provides no lexical information. One way to prove this is to try and find a synonym for #2's does. None can be found. Compare #2's does with #3's below:

3. Janice also does the dishes faithfully.

Here, does = 'washes', so since a synonym has been found, the verb does is not a dummy verb in this sentence.

There is yet another way English can emphasize the action of the verb: by **avoiding contractions** and then **vocally stressing** one of the two elements—the verb form itself, or the negative not—that would have entered into the contraction. Examples:

UNEMPHATIC [with contraction]:
1. Muriel can't practice her cello tonight.

EMPHATIC [without contraction; the vocally-stressed element appears
in bold type with an acute accent mark]:
2. Muriel **cán**not practice her cello tonight.
3. Muriel can **nót** practice her cello tonight.

EXERCISE 3.3

(A) Make emphatic items unemphatic and vice versa. Then read both the emphatic and the unemphatic versions out loud, rendering them both appropriately.

1. We can **not** stand pat.

2. They don't like to see him die.

3. We **will** fight them on the beaches.

4. She's sick and tired of all that.

5. Why **are** we in Samoa?

6. Someone's knocking at my door.

7. They've done everything possible to hurt us.

8. She'd tried to make him behave.

9. She'd try to make him behave if you only let her.

10. I won't put up with you anymore.

11. Do you have any bread?

12. Janice always does what she is told.

(B) Read each of these sentences out loud, stressing, in turn, every word in the sentence. (Thus you will read sentence #1 five times and #2 four.) Then explain the difference between each of the several versions of what you have read aloud.

1. I know why you failed.
2. Italians love grandiose operas.

Contractions: A Summing Up

As is well known (and as the many examples from the previous sections have made clear), English loves to contract. Yet even in English there are limits to contraction.

Most contractions involve not or the auxiliaries—modal and non-modal alike. We will start our discussion with not and how it can and cannot enter into contractions.

NOT

Not contracts by dropping the vowel; the result is n't in writing, which is sometimes pronounced [nt] with [n] as the syllabic nucleus. (In rapid speech, the [t] is often dropped, leaving the syllabic nucleus [n] as the remnant.) When not contracts (and contraction is optional, though frequent in colloquial speech), the contraction **follows** and, in writing, is **attached to**:

(1) all finite forms of the non-modal auxiliaries do/be/have ("finite" here means all forms except the present/past participles and the infinitive); examples:

   DO:
   doesn't   don't   didn't   (cf. *doing't, *done't)
   BE:
   aren't   isn't   wasn't   weren't   amn't [*British English only*]
   HAVE:
   hasn't   haven't   hadn't

(2) all modal auxiliaries (though in some cases the contraction is rare and unusual):

   can't   couldn't   mayn't [very rare]   mightn't
   mustn't   shan't [mainly British]   shouldn't
   won't   wouldn't

(3) some of the peri-modals such as ought (to) and used to:

   oughtn't   usedn't to [very rare]

THE AUXILIARIES

Many of the auxiliaries also form contractions in a variety of verb tenses. They do so by attaching their contracted forms to the end of nouns and to the end of pronouns whether they be personal, possessive, or indefinite.

Contracted auxiliaries also attach themselves to the end of wh words and to here/there. Of course not all auxiliaries enter into all possible contractions, as certain constraints do exist. Note also that auxiliaries **do not form contractions at the ends of clauses or sentences**; thus "He's ready when I'm ready" is grammatical but "*He's ready when I'm" is not. (By contrast, the negative not can indeed appear in clause or sentence-final position: "I can but he can't.")

NON-MODAL AUXILIARY CONTRACTIONS: POSSIBILITIES AND CONSTRAINTS

BE: contracts widely in its present-tense forms

present tense and present progressive

I'm
you're ("You're running scared today"; cf. the possessive
　　determiner your: "Your running scared them")
he's
she's
it's ("It's very hot today"; cf. its as a possessive determiner/
　　pronoun: "The cat lost its bell")
we're ("We're going to leave"; cf. were as a past tense form
　　of be: "We were going to leave")
they're ("They're leaving on the next plane"; cf. their, a pos-
　　sessive determiner: "Their leaving on the next plane
　　worries me")
no one's ("He says that no one's home right now"; cf. the
　　genitive construction no one's, as in "No one's home
　　should be set on fire")
somebody's ("Somebody's very angry at you"; cf. the geni-
　　tive construction somebody's, as in "Somebody's car
　　got stolen")
here're ("Here're the people I told you about")
when's ("When's the plane leaving?")
　　　　etc.

past tense, past progressive, etc.

BE **never** forms contractions of its past tense forms was and were because the contractions they would form—'s, 're respectively—have already been "claimed" by BE's present-tense forms is and are in contraction, so the result would be confusion.

DO: contracts only infrequently

present tense

do offers no contractions of its present tense forms except does, which contracts with what/when/where/who/why/how in very colloquial speech:

"What's he do for a living?"
"When's he usually get home?"
"Where's he work?"

past tense

No contraction of the past tense form did except with what/when/where/who/why/how in very colloquial speech, e.g., "How'd he learn her name?", "Where'd he go to school?"

HAVE: contracts with practically everything

present perfect, present perfect progressive (and, more rarely, **present;** that is to say, the auxiliary have contracts at will, while the LV have seldom does so):

(1) a have contraction is attached to **subject nouns** and to **personal/possessive/indefinite pronouns:**

I've
you've
he's ("He's looked everywhere for the cat" vs.
?"He's no interest in me now"; because the have in this latter sentence is an LV, the sentence is marginally grammatical at best, and would be rejected by many native speakers)
she's ("She's been very helpful to me")
it's ("It's got to be eliminated")
we've
they've
mine's ("Mine's had a lot of problems")
mine've ("Mine've been through all that")
someone's ("Someone's been sleeping in my bed")
etc. [Note that the 's of let's—"Let's all go to the beach!"—contracts us, not has or is.]

(2) a <u>have</u> contraction is attached to all eight <u>wh</u> words—
<u>what</u>/<u>when</u>/<u>where</u>/<u>which</u>/<u>who</u>/<u>whose</u>/<u>why</u>/<u>how</u>/—
and to non-referential <u>there</u> (see ch. 7), especially in rapid
and casual speech. Examples:
> What's he ever done for me?
> Why's he told you so many lies?
> How've they learned English so fast?
> Where've they gone now?
> There's been a lot of trouble there.

MODAL AUXILIARY CONTRACTIONS: POSSIBILITIES AND CONSTRAINTS

Of the nine modal auxiliaries, contractions are mainly made with <u>will</u> and
<u>would</u> (and, less frequently in American English, with <u>shall</u> and <u>should</u>).
<u>Will</u> contracts to 'll, and <u>would</u> to 'd. (Past tense <u>had</u> also <u>contracts</u> to 'd, but
any resultant ambiguity is resolved by other elements in the clause, thus:
"Joe'd been there before" = 'Joe had been there before', since <u>had</u>, not <u>would</u>,
anticipates a past participle as the subsequent verbal element.) Contractions
are attached to all subjects, all interrogative words, and to non-referential
<u>there</u> and <u>here</u> (see ch. 7). Examples:

> John'll be in town tomorrow.
> Anyone'd be able to see he was drunk.
> There'll be all hell to pay.
> Why'd he do a thing like that?

EXERCISE 3.4

(A) Produce contractions wherever possible.

1. You cannot go outside because you will freeze.

2. I would rather have you stay.

3. They have gone and she has returned.

4. I was afraid we were all too tired.

5. He did what he had to do.

6. She doesn't know what time it is.

7. It is time to leave.

8. When is he going to learn whether he has passed?

9. Why did she say she is not sorry?

10. Which will be the one you are going to buy?

11. I would phone them if I could.

12. What does it cost to fly to Buenos Aires?

13. Which are they not planning to take?

14. I am not the kind of guy who will tell a lie.

15. She said that he has an enormous amount of money in the bank.

16. Who does he think he is?

17. Were their children where they were supposed to be?

18. He is insisting that if he had the money he would.

(B) Use each contraction in an original sentence.

    1. Mary'd

    2. I'll

3. they're

4. what's

5. someone'd

6. the dogs've

7. who's

8. sister's

9. which're

10. it's

11. we're

12. what'd

MODALS. PREPOSITIONAL AND PARTICLE VERBS. TRANSITIVITY AND VOICE. CONDITIONALITY.

Modals and Peri-Modals

It should be recalled again that the nine modal verbs can/could/may/might/must/shall/should/will/would are auxiliaries. Non-modals be/do/have are also auxiliaries. One of the topics we will discuss in this section involves the formal and the functional differences between modal auxiliaries and non-modal auxiliaries as well as between both of these together and "main" verbs (LVs)—the vast majority—that are not auxiliaries at all. Mention will also be made of peri[phrastic]-modals, i.e., verb phrases whose behavior is modal-like but only in part.

Consider the following principles:

(1) **Modals take NO *do*-insertion.**

Because they are auxiliaries, modals do not allow do-insertion. The contrasts below exemplify this.

DO-INSERTION: PRESENCE AND ABSENCE

	modal verb: NO do-insertion	main verb: do-insertion needed
+	He can work hard.	He works hard.
–	He can't work hard.	He doesn't work hard.
yn+	Can he work hard?	Does he work hard?
yn–	Can't he work hard?	Doesn't he work hard?
wh/co	Why can he work hard?	Why does he work hard?

(2) **Modals do NOT INFLECT (they lack person, number and tense)**

The following conjugation proves that modals do not inflect whereas LVs do:

I		I	work hard.
You		You	work hard.
He		He	works hard.
She	can work hard.	She	works hard.
It		It	works hard.
We		We	work hard.
They		They	work hard.

(3) **Modals lack past participles and present participles and thus cannot appear in compound tenses.**

Proof of this principle is the fact that the column on the left contains nothing but ungrammatical sentences:

*I have canned work hard.	I have worked hard.
*I can haved work hard.	You have worked hard.
	He has worked hard.
*You have canned work hard.	She has worked hard.
*He has canned work hard.	We have worked hard.

(To express the meaning of can in the past, the perfect tenses, or elsewhere, one must have recourse to the semantically similar perimodal be able to, thus:

I have been able to work hard.
I was able to work hard.
  etc.)

(4) **Modals delete their infinitive complements' to.**

Compare the following grammatical and ungrammatical sentences:

*I can to work hard.	I want to work hard.
I can work hard.	You want to work hard.
	He wants to work hard.

Since can is a modal, any infinitive that follows it as a complement will lose its characteristic to. That is not true of an LV like want, for an infinitive complement following an LV will indeed be marked by to.

(5) **Modals themselves cannot function as infinitives.**

Compare the following grammatical and ungrammatical sentences:

*I want to can do that.	I want to work hard.

The modal in the ungrammatical sentence on the left has sought, unsuccessfully, to function as an infinitive. The only way it can do so is to change from modal <u>can</u> to the semi-auxiliary <u>be able to</u>, as in the following:

I want to <u>be able to</u> do that.

Peri-Modals

Given the many functional limitations on the use of the nine modals <u>can/could</u> etc. (see just above, this chapter), English is fortunate to possess almost two dozen **periphrastic modals** whose functional flexibility is more fully equal to any main verb's. These **peri**[phrastic]-**modals** (so named because they all consist of two or more words and are thus periphrastic) are often divided by linguists into several subcategories variously known as marginal modals, modal idioms, semi-auxiliaries, etc. What all peri-modals have in common is that the first word of each one is either an auxiliary or a modal or marginal modal. In addition, many peri-modals end in the preposition <u>to</u>. Here then are the peri-modals, subcategorized:

THE ENGLISH PERI-MODALS

marginal modals	semi-auxiliaries	modal idioms
ought to	be to	had { better / best
	be { able / about / apt / bound / due / going / likely / meant / obliged / supposed / willing } to	may / might { (just) as well
	(have) got to	would { (just) as soon / rather / sooner
	have to	

Peri-modals cannot take *do*-insertion:

I am about to leave.
*I do am not about to leave. → I am not about to leave.
*Do am I about to leave? → Am I about to leave?
*Don't am I about to leave? → Am I not about to leave?
etc.

Like modals, **marginal modals and modal idioms** do not show person/number/tense:

I ought to take a test.
You ought to take a test.
*He oughts to take a test. → He ought to take a test.
*Yesterday they knew they oughted to take a test.
  → Yesterday they knew they ought to take a test.

However, **semi-auxiliaries** behave like the non-modal auxiliaries they incorporate in that they **do** show person/number/tense:

PERSON AND NUMBER:
  I have got to leave.
  You have got to leave.
  He has got to leave.

  . . .

TENSE:
  Today I have to leave at six.
  Yesterday I had to leave at six.
  I have had to leave at six every day.
  I am having to leave again at six tomorrow.

Marginal modals and semi-auxiliaries retain their to before infinitives, whereas modal idioms are more "modal-like" in the sense that any infinitive following a modal idiom will lose its characteristic to:

MARGINAL MODAL: We ought to stay longer.
SEMI-AUXILIARY: We are supposed to stay longer.
MODAL IDIOM: *We had better to stay longer.
  → We had better stay longer.

Marginal modals and modal idioms cannot function as infinitives, but semi-auxiliaries can:

MARGINAL MODAL: *It's important to ought to work.
MODAL IDIOM: *It's important to had better work.
SEMI-AUXILIARY: It's important to be able to work.

The Meanings of Modals and Peri-Modals

What makes modals and peri-modals interesting linguistically is the extent to which they are **ambiguous semantically**: many have several different meanings. For example, a sentence like

He may work here.

allows for two different interpretations:

> (1) He **has permission** to work here. ["We have done a complete background check on him, have found him satisfactory and have decided to allow him to work here."]

> (2) He **possibly** works here. ["I'm really not sure whether he works here, but it is possible that he does."]

In similar fashion, "I should finish this by eight" either means 'I will probably finish this by eight' or 'I am obligated to finish this by eight.' Also "I could do it" may mean (1) I am physically able to do it, or (2) I have been given permission to do it.

What follows is a chart which lists the modals according to the type of modality that each represents. There are eight different types of modality. Paying attention to patterns and clusters will help you learn which modals correspond to which descriptions. Note that each of these five modals—can, could, may, must, should—represents three different modality types, thereby showing a fair amount of overlap, whereas the modals might, shall, will, and would represent just one modality type each.

THE EIGHT MODALITY TYPES AND THEIR REPRESENTATIVE MODALS

the modality types	**the representative modals**
1. physical/mental ability	can could
2. making requests & granting permission	can could may will would
3. possibility	can could may might
4. probability	must
5. supposition or inevitability	should must
6. wishing	may
7. solicitation of opinion	shall should
8. obligation	must should

Here are examples of each type of modality, together with brief commentary. When a peri-modal can substitute for a modal, that fact is noted.

(1) **Physical and/or mental ability.**
    It is often the case that **both** physical and mental ability are involved in an action, e.g., playing baseball. Although modals typically lack tense distinctions, <u>can</u> is often "present tense" and <u>could</u> "past tense" in this modality type. Note for example:

    He says he <u>can</u> lift 300 pounds.
    He said he <u>could</u> lift 300 pounds.

    One way to make the tense distinction more explicit is to use the peri-modal be able to:

    He says he <u>is able</u> to lift 300 pounds.
    He said he <u>was able</u> to lift 300 pounds.

(2) **Making requests or granting permission.**
    In real-life speech, <u>can/could/will/would</u> are used almost interchangeaby in the making of requests, although some of these modals do a better job than others in fostering the impression of politeness.

    Can
    Could $\left.\right\}$ you fix it for me?
    Will
    Would

    It should be noted that "making requests" is limited to yn+, yn– and wh/co structures, since only these constitute questions, not statements. "Granting permission" involves all five type-two modals; there are, of course, certain connotative differences between them, and some are used less frequently than others to grant permission. <u>May</u>, for example, appears to be limited to first-person requests and second-person responses:

    "May I leave now?"—"You may."
    "May you leave now?"—"I may."

    Old-fashioned prescriptive grammars typically insist that only <u>may</u> (and never <u>can/could</u>) function as the modal of request, but contemporary usage does not support that generalization.

(3) **Possibility**
    Consider the following sentence and its options:

    "From the way he acts, he <u>could/may/might</u> be a doctor."
    There is a **substitution test** that allows us to prove that a modal

belongs to this category (#3, "possibility"). The test works like this: if the phrase "BE possibly" is substitutable for <u>can</u>, <u>could</u>, <u>may</u>, or <u>might</u>, then the modal in question expresses possibility; if not, it doesn't. Here is an example:

(1) "From the way he acts, he <u>could</u> be a doctor."
(2) "From the way he acts, he <u>is possibly</u> a doctor."

Thus sentence #1's modal <u>could</u> expresses possibility. The same modal in the following sentence, however, does not:

(3) "He <u>could</u> be a doctor if he wanted to."
(4) *"He <u>was possibly</u> a doctor if he wanted to."

Sentence #3's modal does not pass the "BE possibly" substitution test and so does not express possibility; instead, it expresses type-one modality—physical/mental ability ("He <u>is able to</u> be a doctor if he wanted to").

Of the four modals expressing possibility, <u>can</u> is the least used, and appears limited to set phrases such as "Where <u>can</u> he be?" ('Where is it possible for him to be?').

(4) **Probability**
Consider the following example:

He drives a brand-new top-of-the-line Hupmobile, so he <u>must</u> be ['is probably'] a doctor, a lawyer, or a movie star.

Whenever <u>BE probably</u> substitutes for <u>must</u>, then <u>must</u> expresses probability, not inevitability or obligation.

The following peri-modals also express probability:

$$
\text{She is} \begin{cases} \text{apt} \\ \text{bound} \\ \text{likely} \end{cases} \quad \begin{matrix} \text{to be president, since she is} \\ \text{certainly in charge here.} \end{matrix}
$$
$$\text{has (got)}$$

(5) **Supposition or Inevitability**
The modals <u>should</u> and <u>must</u> express these two types of modality. At least in part, both share a substitution test: "be likely to / be bound to". Thus if the modal <u>should</u> can be substituted by the peri-modals 'be likely to / be bound to', then <u>should</u> is a modal of **supposition** (and not a modal of obligation). Compare #1 and 2:

(1) [**modal of supposition**] I really should ['am likely to/am bound to'] have a good time, since the tour company has taken care of everything.

(2) [**modal of obligation**] I really should ['had better/must/ought to'] go home now, since I've got to make dinner for the kids.

The substitution test for must as modal of **inevitability** involves "be likely to / be bound to" plus "cannot help but / will inevitably". Here are two examples:

"If I see floating angels playing harps, I must be [am likely to be / am bound to be] in heaven."

"All good things must [cannot help but] come to an end."

Do not confuse must expressing **inevitability** with the must that expresses **obligation**, as in this example: [**modal of obligation**] "He must [has got to] finish on time or he will be punished." (Cf. an impossible substitution for that must: "He must [*cannot help but] finish on time or he will be punished.")

(6) **Wishing**

"May you be haunted by a thousand ghosts."
"May we enjoy every minute of our honeymoon."

This modality is limited to expressing—often as either a curse or as a blessing—something you want to happen. The modal is always may, and always appears at the beginning of the clause.

(7) **Solicitation of opinions** (about an intended action)
For one thing, the should that expresses solicitation of opinions always occurs in a question, whether direct or indirect. For another, the solicitation-of-opinions should can be replaced by "Would[n't] it be a good idea if . . .?" or else "Had[n't] I/you/he [etc.] better . . .?" Here is an example:

"Shouldn't I [Hadn't I better] do the dishes?"

(8) **Obligation**
WEAK obligation:
I should go now.
I ought to go now.
MEDIUM obligation:
I'm supposed to go now.
I had better go now.

STRONG obligation:

I <u>must</u> go now.

I <u>have (got)</u> to go now.

As you see, there are two in each subcategory. All modals of obligation express a sense of duty that ranges from weak to strong. Note the gradations of this sense of duty in the following sequence:

(1) I <u>should/ought</u> to mow the lawn (but I'll probably put it off until later).

(2) I <u>had better/am supposed to</u> mow the lawn (and I'm sure I'll get around to it).

(3) I <u>must/have (got)</u> to mow the lawn, so here I go!

EXERCISE 4.1

(A) Describe the modality type—physical/mental ability, making requests/ granting permission, etc.,—of each modal in the following sentences. Prove your point by employing the appropriate substitution test when possible.

1. From the way he dresses he could be anything—cop, horse breeder, mafia chief, linguistics professor. . .

2. It may rain on our parade.

3. May I come in?

4. May all your chidren be psychiatrists

5. If you combed your hair a different way you might have better luck.

6. You should be able to make it as far as Phoenix tonight.

7. I think I may get an A on the next test.

8. Could you please lend me $5,000,000?

9. You must work 80 hours a week if you want a promotion.

10. I can play baseball better than you can.

11. I have no idea who could have killed my uncle Thigbert.

12. Should I buy the white one or the green one?

13. You shouldn't buy anything until you can afford it.

14. Who's at the door? It must be my mother-in-law.

15. Would you please shut up?

(B) Write an original sentence for each of these modals in the indicated modality.

1. <u>may</u> (requesting or granting permission)

2. <u>must</u> (inevitability)

3. <u>should</u> (supposition)

4. <u>should</u> (solicitation of opinions)

5. <u>can</u> (physical or mental ability)

6. <u>could</u> (possibility)

7. <u>must</u> (probability)

8. <u>would</u> (making requests)

(C) Write an original sentence for each of the following modal idioms. Then **explain** each idiom's meaning by **paraphrasing** it.

1. had better

2. would just as soon

3. might as well

4. would rather

5. would sooner

(D) Use such notions as URGENCY and CONVICTION to explain how the following five sentences differ from each other in meaning.

    1. She could stop drinking.
    2. She should stop drinking.
    3. She had better stop drinking.
    4. She must stop drinking.
    5. She **will** stop drinking.

(E) Using the terminology you have learned in this section of the textbook, explain what is wrong with each of the following ungrammatical sentences.

    1. *He knows he musts stop drinking.

    2. *I've come to learn that I should to get as much exercise as possible.

    3. *They don't will come to the party unless I urge them.

    4. *If it's Saturday night, you're mighting be watch TV at home.

    5. *Why did you insist that he oughted to come right home?

Two-Word Verbs: Prepositional Verbs vs. Particle Verbs

English, like all the other Germanic languages, is very fond of what are known as **two-word verbs** in which the first element is a "real" verb form and the second is a short little "function" word. Here are two examples:

(1) They called on their teacher.
(2) They called up their teacher.

Called is the "real" or LV verb form, and on and up are the function words. Words like on and up are normally both prepositions; we know this because they can go in the following slot, in which there appear the usual prepositional indicators of position, time, space, duration, etc. (see ch. 1):

Eloise ran	up	the hill.
	around	
	on top of	
	by	
	below	
	in front of	
	beneath	
	near	
	beside	
	. . .	

However, when participating in a two-word verb construction, **only the word 'on' is a preposition, whereas the word 'up' is something else,** something that for want of a better name we call a **PARTICLE**. We know this is so by comparing the way that on and up behave in the following sentences, where call on means 'to visit' and call up means 'to telephone':

1.a. They called on their teacher.
   *They called their teacher on.
  b. They called up their teacher.
   They called their teacher up.
2.a. They called on him.
   *They called him on.
  b. *They called up him.
   They called him up.
3.a. They called frequently on their teacher.
  b. *They called frequently up their teacher.
4.a. The woman on whom they called was their teacher.
  b. *The woman up whom they called was their teacher.
5.a. On which teacher did they call?
  b. *Up which teacher did they call?

In these examples, call on and call up behave differently. Therefore, we are forced to conclude that each one belongs to a separate category of two-word verbs. Let's look first at call on. The function word on in call on appears syntactically where we expect a preposition to appear, namely, **BEFORE** the noun or pronoun that it governs. (Remember that prepositions enjoy "pre"-position, i.e., position **before** a noun or a pronoun.) We therefore label the two-word verb call on a **prepositional verb**. However, the function word up in call up does **NOT** always appear before nouns or pronouns, so we have to give it another name: **particle**. Thus two-word verbs that behave like call up are termed **particle verbs** (which some linguists also call 'phrasal verbs').

The following material further explains the differences between prepositional verbs and particle verbs.

PREPOSITIONAL VERBS (prep-v)

To simplify, prep-v prepositions **can or must go BEFORE** things, not after things.

1. with a **noun object:**
   The preposition must **go before** the noun object:

   They called on their teacher.
   *They called their teacher on.

2. with a **pronoun object:**
   The preposition must **go before** the pronoun object:
   They called on him.
   *They called him on.

PARTICLE VERBS (par-v)

To simplify, par-v particles must go **AFTER** things, not before (with just one important exception—#1's noun objects, which see).

1. with a **noun object:**
   The particle can **go either after or before** the noun object:
   They called up their teacher.
   They called their teacher up.

2. with a **pronoun object:**
   The particle must **go after** the pronoun object:
   *They called up him.
   They called him up.

Prepositional verbs function in the following three syntactic environments—intrusive adverbs, intrusive relative pronouns, fronted wh-words—but particle verbs do not. (Another way to say this is that prepositional verbs **ACCEPT** adverb intrusion, relative pronoun intrusion, and wh-word fronting, but particle verbs do not.)

3. **adverb intrusion:**
   Adverbs **can** intrude between LV and preposition:
   They called frequently on their teacher.

3. **adverb intrusion:**
   Adverbs **cannot** intrude between LV and particle:
   *They called frequently up their teacher.

(Note that adverbs can indeed appear **elsewhere** with either prepositional or particle verbs, for example: "Frequently they called on their teacher" / "Frequently they called up their teacher", "They frequently called on their teacher" / "They frequently called up their teacher", "They called on their teacher frequently" / "They called up their teacher frequently.")

4. relative pronoun intrusion

In keeping with the rule that prepositions "go **before**," a prep-v's preposition **can precede** an intrusive relative pronoun:

The woman <u>on</u> whom they called was their teacher.

4. relative pronoun intrusion

Particles, however, **cannot** precede an intrusive relative pronoun:

*The woman <u>up</u> whom they called was <u>their</u> teacher.

Note that if no relative pronoun intrudes, prep-v and par-v constructions superficially resemble each other:

The woman they called on was their teacher.
The woman they called up was their teacher.

The above construction involves the phenomenon known as **gapping** in which a deletable element is omitted from surface structure. Even when the particular deletable element—in this case the relative pronoun—is reinstated, the two constructions share a superficial resemblance:

The woman who(m) they called on was their teacher.
The woman who(m) they called up was their teacher.

Only when the function word is **fronted**—moved frontward in the sentence—do the structural differences between prep-vs and par-vs manifest themselves, as we have seen in "the woman <u>on</u> whom they called was their teacher" and "*The woman <u>up</u> whom they called was their teacher."

5. wh-word as a fronted noun-object

When a noun-object <u>wh</u>-word is fronted and thus appears in sentence-initial position, it **can** be preceded by a **preposition**:

<u>On</u> which woman did they call?

5. wh-word as a fronted noun-object

When a noun-object <u>wh</u>-word is fronted and thus appears in sentence-initial position, it can **not** be preceded by a **particle**:

*<u>Up</u> which woman did they call?

Note that prepositions as well as particles can appear in clause-final position in such constructions:

Which woman did they call <u>on</u>?
Which woman did they call <u>up</u>?

General Comments about Prepositional vs. Particle Verbs

At least 75 percent of all two-word verbs are prepositional verbs. Particle verbs, then, are the "marked" or minority category. So here's a good rule of thumb: when you're in doubt, assume that the two-word verb is a prepositional verb unless proven otherwise. (And the best way for you to "prove otherwise" is to apply to the verb any one of the five syntactic environments that we have just finished examining. In particular, try applying the first or "noun-object" environment, for it's always easy to come up with a noun object to complement a transitive verb. [See the next section for a discussion of transitivity.])

EXERCISE 4.2

(A) Tell whether the underlined two-word verbs are prepositional verbs or particle verbs. Support your decision by offering proof, i.e., by citing which of the five construction types discussed above the particular verb appears in.

1. We <u>set up</u> the VCR.

2. That <u>calls for</u> a lot of planning.

3. I'm going to <u>fill out</u> the forms.

4. Let's <u>tear down</u> that shack.

5. I <u>found</u> him <u>out</u>.

6. <u>Go for</u> it!

7. They <u>looked up</u> my name in the directory.

8. She immediately <u>called out</u> the army.

9. I want you to <u>look at</u> my wart.

10. We don't <u>approve of</u> what you are doing.

11. The engineer <u>turned on</u> the switch.

12. That actor really <u>turns</u> me <u>on</u>.

13. Without any warning he <u>turned on</u> me and ended our friendship.

14. He's always <u>invested</u> heavily <u>in</u> California real estate.

15. <u>In</u> what do you expect me to <u>believe</u>?

16. <u>To</u> whom did he <u>turn</u> in his hour of need?

(B) Write an original sentence with each of these two-word verbs. Make sure each sentence contains a direct object as do nos. 1–16 above, e.g.:

"He called on his teacher."
  S   V   **direct object**

1. hand over

2. put out

3. break up

4. see through

5. hold back

6. bring in

7. stay off

8. look out

(C) Explain, using grammatical terminology, what is wrong with the following ungrammatical sentences, and why.

1. *Give back it right now!

2. *They took rapidly over the company.

3. *He laughed us at.

4. *The gangster off whom they bumped was my godfather.

Transitivity: Active Voice, Passive Voice

Most verbs in English (and other languages) are **transitive**, which means that they will or can take a **direct object**.

A **direct object**—noun or pronoun—is **the first recipient of the action of a verb**; thus:

1. Rebecca gave Eliza the money.
   S[ubject] V[erb] Object Object

In sentence #1, money is the first recipient = direct object (DO) because in order for Rebecca to give the money to Eliza, Rebecca must first pick the money up, extract it from her purse, earn it, borrow it, or whatever. Only when she has it in her hand can she then give it to Eliza. Eliza then is the second recipient = indirect object (IO) of the action of the verb. Rebecca, as the one who is performing the action, is termed the **actor** or subject. To review:

Rebecca	gave	Eliza	the money.
subject= **actor**	**verb=** **action**	**IO=** **second** **recipient** **of action**	**DO =** **first** **recipient** **of action**

An **active voice** construction is one in which **the ACTOR is also the GRAMMATICAL SUBJECT** of the sentence. The **grammatical subject** is the noun or pronoun that determines the conjugatable verb form's person and number. For example, when we substitute one grammatical subject (**GS**) for another, the verb form may have to change:

Doug is a dentist.
I am a dentist.
We are dentists.
    etc.

Here is an example of a typical **active voice construction**:

(1) Joe saw Sandy in the library yesterday briefly at 3:30 p.m.

    actor V DO   prepositional   adverb adverb prepositional
    =GS   phrase   phrase

What follows is sentence #1's **passive voice equivalent**:

2.	Sandy	was	seen	by	Joe	in the library	yesterday	briefly	...
	DO= GS	BE —	past part.	by —	actor =agent	prepositional phrase	adverb	adverb	...

agent phrase

In the above passive construction (#2), the DO functions as the GS, while the actor appears in an **agent phrase** which always begins with the preposition by. The active LV verb saw becomes the passive verb form was seen, which consists of (1) the appropriate tense/person/number-bearing form of the non-modal auxiliary be, and (2) the past participle of the LV (in this instance seen). **None of the remaining complements of section (1) are of any importance and do not enter at all into the active-to-passive transformation** save as remnants to be dealt with as an afterthought. (This means that they can be put almost anywhere without affecting the active-to-passive transformation: "Yesterday at 3:30 p.m. Sandy was briefly seen by Joe in the library" / "Sandy was briefly seen yesterday by Joe at 3:30 p.m. in the library," etc.)

A GS may also consist of an **indirect object**, as the following will show:

ACTIVE:	John	gave	Marsha	a ring.
	actor	verb	IO	DO

PASSIVE 1: A ring was given Marsha by John.
   (Here the DO is the GS.)

PASSIVE 2: Marsha was given a ring by John.
   (Here the IO is the GS.)

Just as active-voice sentences allow compound tenses as well as simple tenses, so do passive. However, in real-life usage it is not likely that all possible compound slots are actually filled, as is shown by the following chart (in which the symbol "?" marks tenses that native speakers do not normally use or readily accept as grammatical):

SIMPLE AND COMPOUND TENSES IN THE PASSIVE VOICE

NON-PERFECT/NON-PROGRESSIVE

PRESENT	The cat is eaten by the dog.
PAST	The cat was eaten by the dog.
FUTURE	The cat will be eaten by the dog.

CONDIT.   The cat would be eaten by the dog.

PERFECT

PRESENT   The cat has been eaten by the dog.
PAST   The cat had been eaten by the dog.
FUTURE   The cat will have been eaten by the dog.
CONDIT.   The cat would have been eaten by the dog.

PROGRESSIVE

PRESENT   The cat is being eaten by the dog.
PAST   The cat was being eaten by the dog.
FUTURE   ?The cat will be being eaten by the dog.
CONDIT.   ?The cat would be being eaten by the dog.

PERFECT PROGRESSIVE

PRESENT   ?The cat has been being eaten by the dog.
PAST   ?The cat had been being eaten by the dog.
FUTURE   ?The cat will have been being eaten by the dog.
CONDIT.   ?The cat would have been being eaten by the dog.

The problem, apparently, with the six examples marked by "?" is that their verb phrases are just too long and cumbersome, and English appears to reject that, especially in the perfect progressive tenses.

(A) Identify each of the following sentences as active voice or passive voice. Then transform from active to passive or vice versa. Last, identify **actor, direct object,** and (if applicable) **indirect object** in both the active and the passive sentences, and then indicate the **grammatical subject** in the passive sentences.

1. The burglar killed the policeman standing in front of the tent.

2. A poor little goldfish was swallowed by the drunken frat rat.

3. Nine out of ten doctors recommend camels for desert trips.

4. The conductor gave Janice a golden violin in appreciation of her fifty years with the Milwaukee Symphony Orchestra.

5. Whales are mercilessly hunted by two or three maritime nations.

6. I bought Henry a Scrabble set for Halloween.

7. Julio's father paid for the new car.

8. The horses had been exercised three times that day by the stable girl.

9. I have been chopping down this tree since noon.

10. Martha was selling tickets for the benefit dance.

11. The natives sold Manhattan to Peter Stuyvesant. [Give **two** possible transformations.]

12. Jane was offered a job by the important executive.

(B) Write five original sentences containing transitive verbs in the active voice. Then transform them all into their respective passive equivalents.

1.

2.

3.

4.

5.

(C) Write five original sentences in the passive voice.

1.

2.

3.

4.

5.

Intransitive Verbs and "Voice"

A purely intransitive verb cannot take a direct object. Ever. English does not have many purely intransitive verbs. Here are various examples of some, along with proof of their inherent intransitivity:

<u>come</u>:   Jennifer always comes $\left\{ \begin{array}{l} \text{early} \\ \text{on time} \\ \text{by car} \\ \text{happily} \\ \quad\text{etc.} \end{array} \right\}$.

The words and phrases in brackets are all adverbs which answer questions such as "when" or "how." They are not direct objects, as the failure of the following sentences to accept the passive transformation will show:

*Early is always come by Jennifer.
*On time is always come by Jennifer.
*By car is always come by Jennifer.
*Happily is always come by Jennifer.

Nor can we force a direct object onto the "Jennifer always comes" structures, as the following proves:

*Jennifer always comes   bread
money
sailboat
library
etc.

Other frequently used intransitive verbs include:

<u>appear</u>   <u>fall</u>   <u>go</u>   <u>happen</u>   <u>lie</u>   <u>rise</u>   <u>wait</u>

A strictly intransitive verb can only be used in an active-voice construction. Intransitives never allow passivization, as we have just seen above; since they lack a DO, there is no DO to become the passive equivalent's GS.

Transitive Verbs in Superficially Intransitive Constructions

Just because a transitive verb **can** take a DO does not mean that it is always going to do so. Indeed, many transitive verbs are frequently unaccompanied by DOs, although since all transitive verbs can take a DO, you can always add a DO to the otherwise objectless construction. Here are some examples of transitive verbs which lack DOs but could readily add them:

1. Al drinks from noon until midnight.
   actor   verb   prepositional phrase

   > (We assume that he drinks alcohol, so a DO like vodka or gin can
   > be readily added:
   >> "Al drinks vodka from noon until midnight.")

2. The beggar approached, but then scurried away.
   actor   verb

   > (We assume that the beggar approached someone, perhaps me,
   > you, him, her, or whomever.)

3. Every year charities ask for money, and this year I
   **adverbial   actor   verb   DO   actor
   phrase**

   decided I would contribute.
   verb   actor   modal   LV

   > (We assume that an IO such as people or us or me can be inserted
   > into the first clause   "charities ask us for money"—and that a
   > DO can likewise be inserted into the second clause: "I decided I
   > would contribute money.")

4. The important thing is to win.
   > (". . . win the game" is an easy expansion to imagine.)

Normally Transitive Verbs Used Intransitively

If a normally transitive verb such as open is used in a construction where no
direct object can be added (e.g., "The door opened" or "The cliff moved"),
then such a verb is indeed being used intransitively and the verb must be
classified as intransitive in this particular instance.

EXERCISE 4.4

(A) Write five original sentences with strictly intransitive verbs.

1.

2.

3.

4.

5.

(B) Write five original sentences containing **transitive** verbs that lack direct object complements.

1.

2.

3.

4.

5.

(C) Write three original sentences in which normally transitive verbs are used intransitively, or in which transitive verbs are used in superficially intransitive constructions. Then tell which type of sentence you have written in each instance.

1.

2.

3.

(D) Identify each of the following sentences as active voice or passive voice. Then change them—if possible—from active to passive or vice versa.

1. The paperboy has come for his monthly payment.

2. This perfume gives off a very strange odor.

3. I went away to the seashore last summer.

4. Luella changed a dollar bill at the convenience store.

5. Seventeen books were returned to the library by three delinquent patrons.

6. By this time tomorrow, another ten thousand innocent civilians will have been killed by the marauding army irregulars.

7. By orders of the dictator, several suspected spies were being tortured by the secret police in the basement of the state security building.

8. Anastasia gave birth to a 7 lb. baby girl.

9. We always travel by bus.

10. The content was analyzed for subversive ideas, and several were found.

11. My son is a doctor.

12. John was loved by Marsha until the end of time.

13. I flew a plane all the way from Dallas to Fort Worth.

14. They will no longer tolerate his attitudinizing monologues.

15. Queen Marie was given a diamond tiara by King Karol.

Real-World Use of the English Passive: Pragmatic Constraints and Agent-Clause Addition

In real-life usage, by no means all passive sentences replicate the "GS + be + past participle + agent phrase" model that we established above. Studies show that **most English passive sentences do not contain an agent phrase**. Thus it is far more common to find sentences such as these—

1. After the tests were graded, the results were posted on the door.

than something such as:

2. After the tests were graded by the professor, the results were posted on the door by her.

One problem with #2 is its clunky style: it is too wordy and too repetitious (there are two agent phrases and two be + past participle phrases). Another problem is that in #2 one can easily figure out who the agent is from context, so any explicit mention of agent comes across as redundant. In all likelihood, #2 would either be expressed in the active voice ("After the professor graded the tests, she posted the results") or would be left to stand as is—as an agentless passive. Agentless passives are useful because they enable us to focus on an IO or a DO—in this case the tests—rather than on the actor/agent as GS. In some instances the agent is simply unknown or not easily determined from context and thus could not be added anyway.

Since the majority of real-life English passive constructions are agentless, the question then becomes: When and why should we add (or retain) an agent phrase? Here are some useful guidelines for doing so:

(1) Add or retain the agent phrase if the agent constitutes **unexpected or surprising information** that the speaker assumes the listener will want to know; thus: "While Jack was walking up the hill, his money belt was ripped off by a sweet little old lady." "A neutron bomb was dropped on Los Angeles yesterday by the Hartzavanian Air Force."

(2) The agent, a specific person—author, painter, composer, inventor, etc.—is simply **too important or too famous** to be omitted: "The opera Turandot was written by Puccini in the early 1920s."

Get Passives

An alternative to passive constructions involving be + past participle are those that involve get + past participle. Thus:

1. Jesse was elected president by a whopping majority.
2. Jesse got elected president by a whopping majority.

While get passives are more limited in function than be passives— for example, get cannot be used with verbs that denote or promote states (*"The answer got understood by everyone")—, their use is widespread, particularly in colloquial English. In most respects, get passives convey the same meaning as their be counterparts; thus:

1. Geraldine was chosen by Walter, not Ronald.
2. Geraldine got chosen by Walter, not Ronald.

However, it is possible that get passives convey a stronger emotional response or a greater sense of finality:

3. René was kicked off the team for smoking.
4. René got kicked off the team for smoking.

get passives take agent phrases even more rarely than do be passives. Another difference between the two is that since get is an LV, not an auxiliary, get requires *do*-insertion in negatives and questions; thus:

	get passive	**be passive**
+	Jerry got caught.	Jerry was caught.
–	Jerry didn't get caught.	Jerry wasn't caught.
yn+	Did Jerry get caught?	Was Jerry caught?
yn–	Didn't Jerry get caught?	Wasn't Jerry caught?
wh/co	When did Jerry get caught?	When was Jerry caught?

Stative Pseudo-Passives

Any stative construction refers to the **result of the action, not the action itself**. The result of an action is the **state** that something is now in (thanks to the action), which is why these constructions are refered to as **statives**. However, they give the appearance of being passives because of the superficial structural similarities between the passive voice construction and the stative construction, as the following will show:

ACTIVE VOICE: The troops surrounded the building.
PASSIVE VOICE: The building was surrounded by the troops.
STATIVE CONSTR.:   The building was surrounded.

In a stative sentence, all action is viewed as being over and done with by the point in time referred to. Since stative sentences necessarily conceive of the action as "already" having happened, it is no surprise that one way to prove whether a sentence is stative is to add the adverb <u>already</u> or the adverb <u>now</u>; if it makes sense, then the sentence is stative. In stative sentences, the verb <u>be</u> is synonymous with <u>remain</u> or <u>stand</u>.

Consider the following <u>narrative</u>, which includes both a passive and a stative:

> At 4:04 p.m. we learned of a hostage situation at the Belvue Building. The strike force quickly arrived on the scene. The building <u>was surrounded</u> by the strike force in less than three minutes [**passive**]. For three more hours the building <u>was surrounded</u> ['remained' surrounded, therefore **stative**]. But <u>suddenly, two shots were heard</u>. . .

EXERCISE 4.5

(A) Use grammatical terminology to tell what's wrong with the following sentences. Then improve each one by rewriting it.

    1. The orchestra was first criticized by the conductor and was then told by the conductor how to perform the passage.

    2. The travel agent had been instructed by his customer to change the date of departure, but she was subsequently informed by him that it had to be changed again by her to what it first was.

(B) Write five passive-voice sentences containing agent phrases.

    1.

    2.

    3.

    4.

    5.

(C) Write five passive-voice sentences that do **not** contain agent phrases.

    1.

    2.

    3.

    4.

    5.

(D) Use grammatical terminology to explain what's wrong with the following sentences. Then improve them all by rewriting them.

    1. *The story got known by everyone in town.

    2. *If Mrs. Wadsworth buys that vase, it will have gotten owned by every prominent family in Salem.

    3. *Marianne gotn't the flu but Sharon did.

(E) Convert these active-voice sentences into (a) passives and (b) statives.

    1. The Swiss Guards recaptured the Vatican.

       (a)

       (b)

2. The national guard reinforced the local police.

(a)

(b)

3. We sold that stallion to the highest bidder.

(a)

(b)

Conditionality

Conditional sentences typically contain two clauses, one of which—often the first one—begins with if. Thus:

"If I had $2,000,000, [then] I'd buy a house in Paris."

The if clause expresses the **condition** that must be realized before something else can happen. The "something else" is expressed as the **result** in the then clause. (The **result** is what would happen were the condition to be realized.)

There are three major types of conditional sentences. Each can be distinguished from the others by the extent to which the information in the if clause is true, hypothetical, or false. The following diagram sums up the major types of conditionality and their subcategories:

THE VARIOUS TYPES OF CONDITIONALITY

(1) TRUE			(2) HYPOTHETICAL		(3) FALSE
(a)	(b)	(c)	(a)	(b)	
eternally	habitually	presumably	more likely	less likely	

We will now explain and exemplify each of the types.

(1) **TRUE.**
This means that the information contained in the if clause is true, whether it is **eternally true** ('true the way a law of science is true'), **habitually true** ('true—often for one particular individual—on a regular, repeated basis'), or **presumably true** (i.e., we presume that the information in the if clause is true because someone has said it was [though at times we only have that someone's word for it]). Here are some examples:

1.a. eternally true:
If you freeze water, it is no longer liquid.
If the moon blocks the sun's rays, an eclipse occurs.
1.b. habitually true:
If I start to cry, you always get mad.
If Kathy calls Tom, he drops everything and runs to her side.
1.c. presumably true:
If you passed the exam, then why are you still studying for it?
If you have an ulcer, do you think it's wise to eat chocolate and drink coffee?

In 1.a. and l.b., the word <u>when(ever)</u> can be substituted at will for <u>if</u> ("Whenever you freeze water, it is no longer liquid", "Whenever I start to cry, you always get mad"). In 1.a., b., and c. alike, the order of the two clauses can readily be reversed ("Do you think it's wise to eat chocolate and drink coffee if you have an ulcer?"). While the <u>if</u> clauses of the 1.a.-type sentences are usually expressed in the present tense, 1.b.-type sentences allow the past tense as well ("If I started to cry, you always got mad"), and 1.c. allows a wide range of tenses ("If you will have finished your book by July, then why would you be afraid to make plans to fly to New York in December?"). Note that 1.c.-type sentences' result clauses often constitute questions ("If you passed . . . then why are you still studying . . .?") but not always, as this example shows: "If you are happily married then you shouldn't be cheating on your spouse."

(2) **HYPOTHETICAL.**

The word <u>hypothetical</u> comes from <u>hypothesis</u>, 'a proposition assumed as a premise; a contingency or conjecture'. In hypothetical conditional sentences, the <u>if</u> clause expresses events or states that may or might possibly happen, and the result clause tells what will occur provided that the <u>if</u> clause's contingency comes true. Thus:

> If you get a haircut, I'll buy you a motorcycle.
> If he eats up all his spinach, we will let him have three helpings of chocolate ice cream.

In effect, the motorcycle is contingent (dependent) on the haircut, as is the ice cream on the spinach: if the one doesn't happen, the other won't either; if the hypothesis remains unrealized, the result will not be forthcoming.

A "prediction scale" applies to hypothetical sentences, as the following will show:

(a) If it snows, the whole city will be paralyzed.
(b) If it {were to / should happen to} snow, the whole city would be paralyzed.

Sentence (a)'s hypothesis—a snowfall—comes across as being more to happen than sentence (b)'s; hence the distinction our diagram makes between "more likely" and "less likely." It should be emphasized that this distinction is not absolute, but one of degrees. Note the following, in which in both the <u>if</u> clause and the result clause a deft use of tenses, modals and adverbs allows us to **proceed from the very likely to the very unlikely**:

VERY LIKELY: 1. If I kill you, I will be free to marry Helen.
               2. If I killed you, I would be free to marry H.
               3. If I were to kill you, I would be free to marry H.
               4. If I should happen to kill you, I would be free to marry H.

VERY UNLIKELY: 5. If ever I should happen to kill you, I would be free to marry H.

Type Two conditionality **always refers to if-clause actions or states that are FUTURE**, i.e., that have yet to be realized. That characteristic differentiates them from Type One conditionals, whose if-clause actions or states are already facts because they have always happened or existed, regularly happen or exist, or are presumed to do so. Compare:

1. If it rains heavily, the valley floods.
   (TYPE ONE conditionality—"true/habitual.")
2. If it rains heavily, the valley will flood.
   (TYPE TWO conditionality—[likely] hypothetical.)

(3) **FALSE.**
False hypotheticals' if clauses contain statements that are contrary-to-fact, i.e., not true. Thus:

"If I had four legs, I could canter like a horse," said the boy.

(Obviously the boy is a human, not a quadriped, so the statement in the if clause—"I had four legs"—is false. Compare the sentence above to the following sentence: '"Before I got caught in the trap and when I still had four legs, I won many races at the dog tracks," said Spot.')

"If they hadn't been driving 95 miles an hour, they would have survived the crash."

(But they **were** driving that fast, so the statement "They hadn't been driving..." is negated, i.e., declared false.)

Type Three conditionals whose if clause verb forms are in the (simple) past tense can sometimes be misclassified as Type Two; thus:
"If I had $200, I'd buy a new bicycle."

If we interpret this as 'If I were to have ['get ahold of'] $200, ..." then the conditionality is hypothetical ("I don't have

$200 but it's possible for me to get it"). But if we interpret the sentence as contrary-to-fact—the speaker doesn't have the money at the time this statement is made—then the sentence must be classified as a Type Three conditional. So which is it? To decide, we merely ask: Does the speaker have the money in hand at the time the statement is made? For additional illustration of this distinction, compare the following two sentences:

1. If you took me to the airport [and it's still possible for you to decide to do so], I'd give you a great big kiss. **HYPOTHETICAL**
2. If you had taken me to the airport [but you didn't, and now it's too late], I'd have given you a great big kiss. **CONTRARY-TO-FACT**

(A) Write one original sentence corresponding to each of these descriptions:

1. type 1.a. conditional ("true: eternally")

2. type 1.b. conditional ("true: habitually")

3. type 1.c. conditional ("true: presumably")

4. type 2 conditional ("hypothetical: more likely")

5. type 2 conditional ("hypothetical: less likely")

6. type 3 conditional ("false")

(B) Classify each of the following conditionals.

1. If she had been born and raised in France, she would be speaking French like a native today.

2. Why aren't you president if you're so smart?

3. If the dam bursts, the town will be inundated.

4. If a baby is born to a drug-addicted mother, the baby is drug-addicted itself.

5. If you're so sick with the flu, then what are you doing here on the dance floor?

6. Had he been a nurse, he would have known what to do.

7. If I make a mistake while driving, I never hear the end of it.

8. If I made a mistake while driving, I never heard the end of it.

9. If I were to make a mistake while driving, I would never hear the end of it.

10. If he had become department head, we'd be in a fine mess now.

11. Connie says that if she doesn't get the scholarship, she will hang herself from the nearest lamppost.

12. If a volcano erupts, either lava or volcanic ash pours out.

13. If that volcano erupts, tons of lava will pour out, burying the sleeply little village up the road.

14. If Sara were the empress of China, she would parade around in antique jade and gold brocade.

5

SOME COMPONENTS OF THE
NOUN PHRASE: FORMS AND FUNCTIONS

Person and Number

Nouns (and to a certain extent pronouns) resemble each other in that they can be described in terms of some or all of the following concepts: **person, number, gender, case,** and **definiteness.** Person and number have already been used to discuss verbs' morphology and syntax (ch. 2), but these important concepts bear reviewing here:

PERSON: either **first, second,** or **third—**
first person: the individual(s) speaking, viewed from a personal vantage point: I. we
second person: the individual(s) being spoken to, viewed from the vantage point of the first person
third person: who or what is being spoken about

NUMBER: either **singular** or **plural. Singular** entails one person/ thing/concept and one only. **Plural** entails more than one.

Gender

The concept of **gender** is new to this chapter, and refers either to **natural gender** or to **arbitrary gender.** Natural gender is sex-characteristic-derived gender. For a noun to be categorized as being subject to **natural gender,** the noun must **denote an animal that manifests identifiable sex characteristics**: either male or female. (In practice, such "animals" are limited to human beings and to the larger mammals, like cows, horses, pigs, elk, moose, etc.) In natural gender, then, whether a noun is grammatically masculine or feminine depends on whether the animal the noun refers to is of the male or the female sex. In languages that also assign gender according to **arbitrary gender** criteria, an entity is assigned a gender—"masculine," "feminine" and in some languages "neuter"—for reasons that have nothing to do with the entity's sex, since as the entity is not an animal it doesn't manifest sex characteristics anyway.

In English, only **natural gender** applies, and only the pronoun system is affected by considerations of natural gender. Compare, for example, the way English is affected by gender to the way a language like Spanish is. In Spanish, gender plays a very important role, as the following chart will show:

GENDER: ENGLISH VS. SPANISH

ENGLISH:

The teacher is a very tall man.
The teacher is a very tall woman.

—The definite article the is the same for masculine natural-gendered as for feminine natural-gendered nouns.

—The noun itself—teacher—is invariant in form, since no "ending" (word-final morpheme) marks one noun as masculine and the other as feminine.

—The indefinite article a is the same for masculine as for feminine natural-gendered nouns.

—The adjective (see ch. 6) has the same form for masculine as for feminine natural-gendered nouns.

SPANISH:

El maestro es un señor muy alto.
La maestra es una señora muy alta.

—The definite article assumes one form—el—if the noun it modifies is masculine (maestro '[male] teacher' and thus masc.-gendered for reasons of natural gender) and another form—la—if the noun it modifies is feminine (maestra '[female] teacher').

—The noun itself is marked as masculine (by the bound inflectional morpheme /o/ at its end) or feminine (by /a/ at end).

—The indefinite article assumes one form—un—if the noun it modifies is masculine and another form—una—if the noun it modifies is feminine.

—The adjective assumes one form —alto— if the noun it modifies is masculine and another form—alta—if the noun it modifies is feminine.

Note that while each of the Spanish sentences tells us no less than five times that the head noun maestro/maestra is masculine or feminine, each English sentence does so only once—with the sentence's respective head noun. In English, the **pronoun system** is a much better illustration of the interface between considerations of natural gender and considerations of form. All pronoun forms marked for gender appear in bold type.

(GENDER MARKING AND) THE ENGLISH PERSONAL PRONOUN SYSTEM

subjects		objects		possessives			
				determiners		pronouns	
I	we	me	us	my	our	mine	ours
you	you	you	you	your	your	yours	yours
he	they	**him**	them	**his**	their	**his**	theirs
she	they	**her**	them	**her**	their	**hers**	theirs
it	they	it	them	its	their	its	theirs

Case

Case, first explained in ch. 1, makes itself manifest in the table that has just been presented. By **case** we mean the different functions that a form performs, and also the differences in form as these are determined by function. **Case** then differs from both **form** and from **part of speech**, as the following makes clear:

> **PART OF SPEECH:** as explained in ch. 1, i.e., whether a word functions as a noun, a pronoun, an adjective, a verb, an adverb, a preposition, etc.
>
> **CASE:** whether a particular part of speech—for example a noun—is the genitive, the subject or the object of the sentence it appears in, or, if the object, whether it is the direct object or the indirect object.
>
> **FORM:** the collection of morphemes within a word and how they are arranged to bring about meaning. (What come quickest to mind are the examples from ch. 2: morpheme /z/ and morpheme /d/ and their various allomorphs.)

A good illustration of **case** and its interaction with **form** is the entity of "first-person plural pronoun." If 1.pl.'s function is to serve as a **subject**—the doer of the action or the experiencer of the state—then the form that 1.pl. takes is we; if 1.pl.'s function is that of **object**—the recipient or "patient" of the action—, then us is the form that 1.pl. takes. If 1.pl. functions as the expresser of possession (ownership) and stands before the possessed noun (the thing owned), then a **possessive determiner** form is taken, whereas if the indicator of possession constitutes its own noun phrase, then a **possessive pronoun** form is assumed. We/us/our/ours then are the four different **forms** that 1.pl. assumes, depending on what **case** they're in. The following sentences illustrate each one:

> **SUBJECT CASE:**
> I gave Carolyn the money.
>
> **OBJECT CASE:**
> Carolyn gave me the money.
>
> **POSSESSIVE DETERMINER CASE:**
> Carolyn gave my money to charity.
>
> **POSSESSIVE PRONOUN CASE:**
> It was only mine that she gave, not someone else's.

While other persons and numbers can also have four different forms (1.sg., 3.pl.) or three different forms (2.sg., 2.pl., 3.sg. masculine and 3.sg. feminine), some persons and numbers have just two different forms (3.sg. neuter it/its).

Expressing Possession: Genitives and Partitives

When we relate English nouns forms to the cases they serve in, we see that English nouns have only two form-marked cases: **genitive** and **"all other."** The "all other" or unmarked case form is the form that English employs for nouns whenever they are not in the genitive case. The genitive case is most commonly used to express **possession**—X belonging to Y, as in the following:

> Sally's toothbrush
>   Y   X
> Juan's hamburger
>   Y   X

However, the genitive case can also be used to express **length and measure** ("a summer's vacation" [a vacation that lasted all summer]) as well as **purpose** ("the homosexuals' concentration camp" [a concentration camp in which homosexuals were imprisoned]), **origin and agent** ("Tennessee Williams' plays" [the plays written by TW]), and **relationship and association** ("the national park's redwood trees" [the redwood trees in the national park]).

In some instances, a genitive construction can be equated with a **partitive construction**. Partitives use of to express possession while genitives use 's or s'. Here is an example of a genitive and a partitive that mean the same thing and are used with equal frequency:

1. That boy's name is Vincent.
          Y   X
2. The name of that boy is Vincent.
       X   Y

While sentences like #1 and #2 mean the same thing and are used with equal frequency, the same is not true of pairs like the following:

3. My aunt's pen is on my uncle's desk.
4. ?The pen of my aunt is on the desk of my uncle.

Sentence #4 sounds stiff, overly formal, unnatural and even French (as if it were a literal translation of the famous XIXth-century textbook practice sentence La plume de ma tante c'est sur le bureau de mon oncle). When, then, does English prefer (or demand) the genitive and when does it prefer/ demand the partitive to express possession, length, measure, purpose, origin, agent, and so forth? **In general, English prefers the genitive if Y (possessor) is a human being or one of the larger animals, or if Y represents a collective noun where people constitute the collectivity, or if Y operates** through human intervention (though Y may not be human itself). Here are some examples:

GRAMMATICAL	UNGRAMMATICAL
Why don't you take Jane's car?	*Why don't you take the car of Jane?

MORE PREFERED/ MORE FREQUENT	LESS PREFERRED/LESS FREQUENT
He showed me the boy's new bike.	He showed me the new bike of the boy.
Pete stepped on the cat's tail.	Pete stepped on the tail of the cat. ("The Tail of the Cat" sounds like the name of a quaint bar or restaurant.)
The gangster's favorite food is donuts.	The favorite food of the gangster is donuts.
The congregation's budget was being discussed.	The budget of the congregation was being discussed.

As already noted, English also prefers the genitive to the partitive even though the Y possessor is not animate but can be viewed as performing an action that involves a human intermediary. Example:

The plane's landing took place under extremely hazardous conditions.	The landing of the plane took place under extremely hazardous conditions.

But if the Y possessor consists of a **long noun phrase**, it is the **partitive** that is preferred, even though the Y possessor is human:

She is the confidant of that infamous all-controlling university president.	She is that infamous all-controlling university president's confidant.

And only the partitive can be used in expressions of quantity or quality:

UNGRAMMATICAL:	GRAMMATICAL:
*He asked for a coffee's cup.	He asked for a cup of coffee.
*I dislike this investigation's type.	I dislike this type of investigation.

In similar fashion, **non-animate and lifeless possessors clearly insist on the partitive**:

UNGRAMMATICAL:	**GRAMMATICAL:**
*Money's love is all evil's root.	The love of money is the root of all evil.

Unfortunately, no hard and fast rules exist for other types of constructions involving possession. In some cases, selecting genitive or partitive becomes an issue of register—genitive if the usage is informal, partitive if the usage is formal. Here are two examples of that:

INFORMAL REGISTER	**FORMAL REGISTER**
Victor Hugo's novels	the novels of Victor Hugo
Madame Curie's discoveries	the discoveries of Madame Curie

Partitive-Genitive Constructions

A partitive-genitive (par-gen) construction contains **both the partitive of and the genitive 's/s'** in adjacent noun phrases, thus:

1. Any friend **of** Steve**'s** is a friend of mine.
2. A cousin **of** Sara**'s** was accidentally shot at the mall.

By containing both the partitive and the genitive, a par-gen gives the impression of being redundant, for such a construction seems to be marking possession twice—once with 's/s', and again with of. While the constraints on usage of this construction are still not well understood by linguists (thus # 1 can be expressed as a partitive alone, and with no difference in meaning ["Any friend of Steve is a friend of mine"], while # 2 cannot), it is nonetheless the case that in some circumstances a separate par-gen construction is absolutely necessary in order to reflect differences in meaning such as the following:

3. I saw a statue of George Washington.
4. I saw a statue of George Washington's.

Sentence #3 refers to a statue which depicts the likeness of Washington, whereas #4 refers to a statue that once belonged to Washington but does not depict him. Here is another paired sample:

5. They bought a painting of my aunt.
6. They bought a painting of my aunt's.

The par-gen construction requires that the Y possessor be human. Thus we say "I found it in the basement of a friend's" but do not say *"I found it in the basement of a building's."

EXERCISE 5.1

(A) Classify the underlined words as to whichever of the following descriptors apply: **person, number, gender, part of speech,** and **case.**

1. She told him that I killed the cat.

2. Joan's mother's neighbor wanted a wife for her son.

3. As the president was leaving the banquet hall, she ran into a head of state whom she had not yet had an opportunity to say hello to.

4. The principal ordered his subordinates to "get" all teachers who opposed him.

5. We know we will never be defeated by any other men.

6. Did you lose the can of worms or did you throw it out?

7. I heard them when they called us.

8. He saw you as you were leaving me at Joe's Bar last night.

(B) The following sentences are about to be translated into a language whose nouns show both natural and arbitrary gender. Tell which under-lined nouns show natural gender and which ones show arbitrary gender. Explain your decisions.

1. My <u>grandmother</u> sold the <u>house</u> in the <u>city</u> and moved in with my <u>uncle</u>.

2. A <u>psychiatrist</u> stood up and told the <u>speaker</u> off.

3. Many <u>people</u> get lost every <u>year</u> in the <u>subway</u>.

4. The <u>ghost</u> frightened the <u>witch</u> but saved the <u>princess</u> from the <u>dragon</u>.

5. The <u>gentry</u> and the <u>nobility</u> looked down on the <u>serfs</u> and, from the <u>heights</u> of their <u>castles</u> high above the <u>sea</u>, on the <u>surf</u> as well.

6. After killing his <u>master</u> and his <u>mistress</u>, the <u>butler</u> wiped the <u>gun</u> with a <u>handkerchief</u>.

(C) Some of the following sentences use the genitive 's/s' or the partitive of correctly, while others do not. Point out (1) those usages which are flat-out ungrammatical, (2) those which though grammatical are unnatural, and (3) those usages which are both grammatical and natural. Explain your decision in each instance.

1. Rebecca's mother's family's youngest generation all died without heirs.

2. The money of my father will all go to the widow of my brother.

3. Happiness's pursuit is guaranteed by our nation's constitution.

4. The older son of my favorite next-door neighbor turned 21 today.

5. The mob felt that pleasure's seeking was all good's sum.

6. The howling mob's chief goal was to burn down the decadent aristocrat's palace.

7. I disapprove of his thinking's way.

8. According to Sam's expert opinion, the operas of Puccini are the best around.

9. The queen lost it in the attic of the castle's.

10. The sword of the bodyguard of the queen was impaled on the suit of armor of the mysterious and utterly fascinating black knight of song and legend.

(D) Write five original sentences containing correctly used partitive-genitive constructions.

1.

2.

3.

4.

5.

Common and Proper Nouns. Determiners.
Mass and Count Nouns.

All nouns are either **common** or **proper**. In addition, all common nouns must be classified according to whether they are being used as **mass** or as **count** nouns. Knowing whether a common noun is mass or count will enable us to explain how to use **determiners** correctly. Let us now define and explain all these terms and distinctions.

Proper nouns are known colloquially as "names" and do indeed encompass the gamut of first, middle, and last names both human, humanoid, and nonhuman: Billy Bob, Quincy Jones, Sarita Montiel, Wolfgang Amadeus Mozart, Mrs. Grundy, Macchiavelli, Bat Man, Dame Agatha Christie, Darth Vader, Austin Powers, the Empire State Building, the Eiffel Tower, the Taj Mahal, Iguazú Falls, the Rocky Mountains, etc. Singular proper names are pluralized when they refer to copies, imitations ("We've sold out all the Eiffel Towers in our gift store") or successors ("Stanislaw was thrilled to the bone to witness the swift descent to earth of the first of the 57 flying Elvises"). Proper nouns also do not co-occur with **determiners** (a[n]/some/the/this/these/that/those) except when the need arises to distinguish one same-named proper noun from another, or to indicate how extremely important the bearer of the name is. Examples:

1. Vinnie had a run-in with a cop. [no determiner]
2. *The Vinnie had a run-in with a cop. [determiner ungrammatical]
3. The Vinnie from Brooklyn had a run-in with a cop, but the Vinnie from Staten Island did not.

> [determiners used to distinguish between two same-named people]

4. Why, I'll have you know that this particular vampire is **the** Count Dracula, direct from Transylvania.

> [determiner that emphasizes the importance of the bearer of the proper noun]

Common nouns are all nouns that are not proper nouns.

By now it should be clear what is meant by **determiners**, which are listed and labeled systematically below:

THE DETERMINERS OF ENGLISH

ARTICLES

   DEFINITE:

   the [which co-occurs with both singular and plural nouns]

INDEFINITE:

a, an   [both are singular only]
some   [if used as an article, some typically co-occurs with plural nouns]

1. I wanted a pear but I bought an apple.
2. The store had some pears that I wouldn't touch with a ten-foot pole.

DEMONSTRATIVES

	SINGULAR:	PLURAL:
close to speaker	this	these
close to hearer/	that	those
far from both hearer		
and speaker alike		

We combine articles and demonstratives under the single classifying term **determiners** because articles and demonstratives behave similarly: both precede nouns, neither takes the comparative or the superlative forms that adjectives (ch. 6) take, and neither one of them behaves like adjectives in any other ways either.

As previously noted, all common nouns function in any given context either as **mass nouns** or as **count nouns**. A count noun is **any noun that allows pluralization and can be modified by plural numbers—two, nine, 327, etc.—or by quantity words such as many.** A mass noun on the other hand does not allow pluralization and is modified by quantity words like much or by measure words or phrases like a cup of or a piece of. The table that follows sets forth the relationships between mass noun and count noun usage in all possible environments involving determiners or their absence. When using this table, put it into the wider context of English in general and the hundreds of thousands of English nouns by keeping this in mind: **while nearly all nouns can function as count, only a handful can function as mass. "Mass" then is the marked, minoritarian or elite category.**

THE MASS NOUN/COUNT NOUN DISTINCTION:
POTENTIAL ENVIRONMENTS

	∅[no determiner]	the	a(n)	some
SINGULAR	a	c	e	g
PLURAL	b	d	[f]	h

Our archetypical **mass** noun is meat. Any noun which behaves like meat is functioning as a mass noun.

Our archetypical **count** noun is husband. Any noun which behaves like husband is functioning as a count noun.

Mass	Count
a. Meat is good for you.	a. *Husband washes the dishes.
b. *Meats are good for you.	b. Husbands wash the dishes [while wives dry them].
c. The meat looks good to me [so go ahead and eat it, but don't eat the cheese, which is moldy].	c. The husband washes the dishes [and the wife takes out the garbage].
d. *The meats are good for you.	d. The husbands wash the dishes [and the wives dry them].
e. *A meat is good for you.	e. A husband washes the dishes [whereas a wife dries them].
f. --------	f. --------

(Note: by definition, no **singular** indefinite article could ever co-occur with a **plural** noun, so environment f is an impossibility.)

g. Some meat is good for you.   g. Some husband washes the dishes.
(Note: both g-mass and g-count need additional explanation. G-mass uses some not as an indefinite article but as a quantity word: here, some 'a certain amount of'. G-count employs some in a special, almost idiomatic fashion to mean 'any anonymous and unimportant entity'. "Some husband washes the dishes" would appear in a context similar to the following: "As the movie starts, boring married people stand in a kitchen doing various things: some wife is basting a turkey, some husband is washing the dishes . . .")

h. Some meats are good for you [whereas others aren't]. (Note: h-mass is an example of **mass-to-count shift**, which we will examine shortly.)	h. Some husbands wash the dishes [whereas others don't].

Nouns functioning as **mass** never pluralize. (Example h has already been identified as a mass-to-count shift, so in h, the mass noun meat is now a count noun.) Nouns functioning as **mass** never co-occur with the singular indefinite article a. Mass nouns, then, are limited in function to these environments:

—no determiner / singular [environment a]
—definite article / singular [environment c]●●●
—some / singular [environment g]●●●

Count nouns' environmental spread is much greater. Count nouns occur in **all environments except** Environment 'a', "no determiner / singular." Here is a list of the environments in which count nouns occur:

—no determiner / plural [environment b]
—definite article / singular [environment c]●●●
—definite article / plural [environment d]
—indefinite article / singular [environment e]
—some / singular [environment g]●●●
—some / plural [environment h]

Note the ●●● symbols. They mark the only two environments—c and g—in which mass nouns and count nouns can overlap. (In all other environments, mass and count are mutually exclusive.)

Mass-to-Count Shifts

As noted above, most nouns that typically function as mass can also function as count. They can do so when denoting either (1) 'a type, kind or brand of' something, or (2) 'a portion, a serving or a unit of' something. The following illustrates the mass-to-count noun shift:

MASS: —————————————➤ **COUNT:**

cheese:
    Cheese is made from milk.   France produces about 500 different cheeses.

gas:
    Gas costs relatively little in some countries.   Hydrosalostrontium is a gas that is deadlier than any other. Among all the gasses in the world, only baccilosalate approaches it in force.

milk:
    Milk comes from cows, goats, and other mammals.   I want three donuts and a milk to go.
There are so many milks on the market today that it's practically impossible to choose.

chocolate:
    Chocolate ranges in color from light brown to pitch black.   That box contained some chocolates that I just couldn't resist.

As can be seen, many of the essentially mass nouns that can also be used as counts involve food or liquid.

Dual-Function Nouns: Nouns That Are Both Mass and Count

A few English nouns—often those which express abstract concepts—function perfectly well in both categories: as either mass or count. A good example is the noun sin. The following order of presentation is identical to the one used above (see p. 171).

(see p. 171)

MASS:	COUNT:
a. Sin is very serious if allowed to go unpunished.	a. --------
b. --------	b. Sins of that sort are very serious if allowed to go unpunished.
c. The sin of adultery is very serious.	c. The sin he committed yesterday is very serious.
d. --------	d. The sins he committed yesterday are very serious.
e. --------	e. A sin such as adultery is very serious.
g. Some sin is very serious.	f. I hear he committed some sin or other.
h. [mass-to-count shift]	g. Some sins are very serious.

In general, sin as a mass noun means 'sin in general', while sin as a count noun equals 'an individual occurrence of sin'. Other nouns which like sin are dual-function include death, crime, beauty, life, truth, and education.

Definiteness and Specificity

Nouns which co-occur with indefinite articles are either non-specific or specific. If the indefinite article + noun refers to an entity that is unknown to either the speaker or the hearer, that noun is non-specific in the sense that its referentiality has yet to be established: it could refer to anyone or anything. But if either the speaker or the hearer possesses knowledge of the entity, then it is specific. Consider the following:

1. Stanley wanted to marry a Czech, but as he didn't know any, he hopped on the next plane to Prague to see if he could meet one. [The clause beginning with but tells us that the Czech mate is strictly hypothetical at this point, so "a Czech"'s indefinite article a must be labeled **non-specific**.]

2. Stanley wanted to marry a Czech, but his old-country Slovak great-grandmother took one look at her and said, "No way, José." [Here, "a Czech" refers to **an entity that the narrator knows or has heard about** and that the

subject of the first clause—Stanley—has obviously come to know as well. "A Czech" in sentence 2, then, is clearly **specific**.]

Nouns co-occuring with **definite articles** are **always specific** in the sense that their referentiality is assumed to be known to both speaker and hearer alike. Thus:

3. So when Stanley finally had to tell the Czech he couldn't marry her because of his great-grandmother's disapproval, she bounced right on back to Prague and married someone else.

EXERCISE 5.2

(A) Identify all nouns in the following sentences. Then classify each one as **proper or common** and also (if common) as to how it is functioning in the particular sentence—as **mass or count**.

1. John and Marsha bought a house last year in Rego Park.

2. It had a basement so they made wine there and then stored it in the darkest corner possible.

3. I want chicken for dinner tonight.

4. The chickens were killed on the chopping block.

5. Marsha plucked their feathers, then spilled their guts into the garbage can and rapidly washed her hands three times.

6. The theory cannot be proven by any professor.

7. Some fish is what Priscilla would like for the picnic.

8. So then some fish jumped into Jennifer's net and said, "Well hi there!"

9. It then tried to get some honey, but was stung by some bees.

10. Several different types of tea are imported from China.

11. The teetotaler said he would like a lemonade.

12. Some unopened Cokes were left behind at the picnic site.

(B) Write one original sentence corresponding to each of the following descriptions.

1. <u>beer</u> as a count noun

2. <u>beer</u> as a mass noun

3. any singular count noun co-occurring with an indefinite article

4. any mass noun not co-occurring with a determiner

5. any plural count noun co-occurring with <u>some</u>

6. any plural count noun not co-occurring with a determiner

7. any mass noun co-occurring with a definite article

8. any plural count noun co-occurring with a definite article

9. any plural count noun co-occuring with an indefinite article

10. a dual-function noun which functions here as count

(C) Fill in the blanks with either <u>much</u> or <u>many</u>.

1. I don't have _____ time left.

2. _____ effort has been expended on this project.

3. He said that _____ workers felt just the way he did.

4. I wanted to tell him that _____ attention was being paid to the problem.

5. Now is the time for _____ good men to come to the aid of the hurricane victims.

6. However, _____ people wouldn't agree with you.

7. The important thing is for _____ money to be spent.

8. _____ loving care is also needed.

9. But so are _____ millions of dollars.

(D) Identify the following sentences' determiners as either **specific** or **non-specific**.

1. The teenage girl had no idea what to buy for Mothers' Day, so she went looking for a compact disc that wasn't too expensive.

2. She found a disc of the loveliest Bulgarian opera she had ever heard.

3. However, a disc like that cost a fortune, so she bought her mother a CD of rap music by the group "2 Dead 2 Croak."

4. In consequence, her mother had quite a surprise awaiting her, and she returned the disc to the store the very next day.

Pronouns

According to the sort of grammar that one studies in the lower grades, pronouns are words that "can replace or refer back to nouns or noun phrases." However, this definition is flawed. Consider the following example sentence:

1. Ramón bought a sandwich, then he ate it.

As sentence #1 contains no other antecedent for he than Ramón, it is safe to assume that 'he' is **co-referential** to Ramón. (**Co-referential** means that two lexical items refer to the same entity—in this case he and Ramón to each other. Ramón comes first, so it is antecedent; he, coming second, is subsequent; the same comments are valid for sandwich and it.) In a sentence such as the following, however, he has the potential to refer to an antecedent located in any sentence coming before it:

2. Ramón had to go home because he got sick.

When sentence #2 stands alone, he and Ramón are likely co-referentials. But consider the following two expanded contexts:

3. Ramón and Gilbert had planned to stay at Joe's house until Monday, but suddenly Gilbert experienced severe stomach cramps, so Ramón had to go home because he got sick.

In sentence #3, he clearly refers to Gilbert, not Ramón. In the next sentence, however:

4. Ramón, who has a long history of gastroenteritis and its related problems, had to go home because he got sick.

he can only refer to Ramón, regardless of whatever information might get added to the context in a foregoing sentence.

Another reason why the lower-grade rule about pronouns replacing nouns is flawed can be seen by analyzing the following two sentences:

5. The monster screamed and you kept on screaming.
6. The drivers were dizzy so we got out and lay down.

While these two sentences are grammatical, they strike us as more than a little bit illogical: we expect the monster to keep on screaming in sentence #5, and the driver to get out and lie down in sentence #6, but for either of those events to happen, the pronouns in the second part of each sentence would have to be different—"[the monster screamed and] it kept on screaming" in #5, and "[the drivers were dizzy, so] they got out and lay down" in #6. The fact is that neither #5's you nor #6's we has any antecedent. This fact draws our attention to a general rule about pronouns and co-referentiality: **only THIRD-PERSON pronouns replace nouns or noun phrases.** So if we define pronouns as "words which can replace nouns" etc., we exclude all first- and second-person pronouns, which is something we obviously cannot do. So the only solution is to say that since first- and second-person "pronoun" forms behave (morphologically and syntactically) exactly like third-person pronouns, then first- and second-person forms might as well be considered pronouns too, even though they're never actually "pro" ['in place of'] anything.

Those sets of pronouns which for the most part refer to humans are traditionally termed **personal pronouns**, even though one of them—it— never refers to humans, and the third-person plural personal pronoun forms can be either human or nonhuman in their referentiality, according to context, as the following example shows:

1. Those nasty boys got what they had coming to them.
vs.
2. The eggs were a mess: their shells were all cracked, and they lay on the floor as the crowd stepped all over them.

Personal pronoun forms typically reflect differences in **case**; thus for many personal pronoun person/number configurations there are different forms for subject, for object, for possessive determiner and for possessive pronoun, as the following chart will show. (This chart is the same one that was presented earlier, on p. 160.)

THE ENGLISH PERSONAL PRONOUN SYSTEM

subjects		objects		possessive determiners		possessive pronouns	
I	we	me	us	my	our	mine	ours
you	you	you	you	your	your	yours	yours
he	they	him	them	his	their	his	theirs
she	they	her	them	her	their	hers	theirs
it	they	it	them	its	their	its	theirs

It will be recalled—see pp. 17, 161—that a **subject** is what governs verb agreement, serves as the antecedent for a regular tag question, and is the first noun phrase to the left of the auxiliary or the conjugated main verb in a non-inverted sentence. An **object**, whether **direct** or **indirect**, is the recipient of the action of a transitive verb. Not yet defined are the two types of **possessives**. A **possessive determiner** is given that name because it functions syntactically like the other types of determiners—articles and demonstratives—that we have already examined, and appears before the noun phrase it forms part of (thus: "I lost the/a/that/my new coat yesterday"). A **possessive pronoun** behaves in a co-referentially pronominal fashion, replacing or referring back to a noun or noun phrase in the following manner:

Sandy lost her coat yesterday and I lost mine on Sunday.

The Morphology of Personal Pronouns

Even a quick glance at the personal pronoun chart we have just presented shows that one cannot always determine **case** from form alone; thus the form you can be either subject or object, as can it, and two of the three third-person singular possessives can function as determiners or pronouns alike; in similar fashion, her is either an object or a possessive determiner according to context (**object**: "I saw her today"; **possessive determiner**: "I saw her mother today").

Of the 25 distinct personal pronoun forms filling 40 separate slots on the foregoing personal pronoun chart, you is the most ubiquitous, filling four slots: 2.sg. and 2.pl. subject, and 2.sg. and 2.pl. object. This lack of distinctiveness has brought about a wide variety of popular spoken forms in the 2.pl. slots (both subject and object) in popular speech: you-all and y'all (not to be confused with you'll), youse, youse guys, you guys (applied indistinctively to both men and women), you'ns ('you ones') and (in British English) you lot.

Morphologically, possessive determiners can be distinguished from possessive pronouns by the word-final /s/ in all but one instance (1.sg.). The rule is this: to all determiner forms except my, add /s/ to create the pronoun equivalent unless an /s/ ends the form already (as it does in his and its).

Reflexive Pronouns

Their forms are as follows.

	singular	plural
first person	myself	ourselves
second person	yourself	yourselves
third person masculine	himself	themselves
third person feminine	herself	themselves
third person neuter	itself	themselves

With two exceptions, English reflexive pronouns are formed by combining a possessive determiner with -self if singular or with -selves if plural; thus my + self, her + self, etc. The two exceptions are himself and themselves, in which the first element of the compound is the **object** form and not the possessive determiner. (In some lects of spoken English, however, the regularizing and highly stigmatized hisself and theirselves/theyselves do indeed occur.)

Reflexive constructions expressing reflexive concepts involve an object [usually direct] which is co-referential to the clause's subject. Thus, subject and object are identical in reference. Examples:

1. Jim shot himself. [= Jim$_1$ shot Jim$_1$]
2. Jackie made herself some eggs. [= Jackie$_1$ made eggs for Jackie$_1$]
3. The goatherds threw themselves from the cliff.
     [= The goatherds$_1$ threw the goatherds$_1$ from the cliff]
4. Jane hates herself. [= Jane$_1$ hates Jane$_1$]
5. Why, we just love ourselves to death! [= We$_1$ love us$_1$ to death]

English reflexivity can be confusing in the sense that English allows **reflexive concepts** (subject and object co-referentiality) to be expressed with **non-reflexive constructions** which lack reflexive pronouns. Compare:

6. François shaved rapidly.
7. François shaved himself rapidly.

In general, the English rule is this: if it is clear who the reflexive object is— himself in #7—then it can be deleted (as in #6). It is often the case that a reflexive concept finds itself expressed with a two-word verb (pp. 121–24) or with a <u>got</u> construction as the following show:

8. Sue got up and got dressed in a hurry.
9. All of a sudden Jerry got very sleepy so he lay down and took a nap.

Indeed, certain reflexive concepts appear to reject the reflexive construction altogether, as can be seen in the following:

10. *Sue arose herself and dressed herself in a hurry.
     [The phrase <u>dressed herself</u> is acceptable, though formal, but *<u>arose herself</u> is simply ungrammatical, at least in modern English.]
11. *All of a sudden Jerry ensleepened himself so he reclined himself and took a nap.
     [There simply is no such verb as <u>to ensleepen (oneself)</u>, and <u>to recline (oneself)</u> sounds odd at best.]

Some reflexive constructions actually do not express reflexive concepts. What they express instead is emphasis and/or exclusivity, as #12 and 13 show:

12. The owner himself built the house. [= The owner built the house—no one else did so.]
13. The owner built the house himself. [= Essentially the same meaning as # 12.]

In theory, a single clause could contain two reflexive pronouns—one used for emphasis and the other for co-referentiality:

14. Joe himself shaved himself.

However, such a construction though grammatical is awkward, and is more likely to be expressed as follows:

15. Joe shaved all by himself [i.e., today was the first time that this young adolescent succeeded in shaving himself unaided].

Reciprocal Constructions

Reciprocity means **mutuality of action**: A does to B what B does to A. The phrases each other and one another are used to represent it. Thus:

1. John and Marsha love each other.

(An underlying representation of this would be: John loves Marsha and Marsha loves John.)

2. Connie and Sandy would always help one another study for tests.

A constraint on reciprocity is that **reciprocal pronouns must appear in the same clause as their antecedents:**

3. *Rich said that Joe thought highly of each other.

Sentence #3 is ungrammatical because it contains two clauses—"Rich said [something]" and "Joe thought highly of [someone]"—and the first antecedent (Rich) appears in clause one while the second (Joe) appears in clause two. For # 3 to be grammatical, it must change to read:

4. Rich and Joe thought highly of each other. [This sentence consists of one clause only:

Rich and Joe	thought	highly . . .	
subject	**verb**	**adverb**	**complements**]

EXERCISE 5.3

(A) Identify and describe all personal, reflexive and reciprocal pronouns in the sentences below. Specify their **case**. Whenever possible, mention **person, number, and gender**.

1. Perry and Bill packed their bags and took them to the airport so as not to miss their flight.

2. Sally says she saw her sister Sue save herself a slice of salami.

3. Have you seen your father lately?

4. What's mine is mine, and what's yours is yours.

5. All my friends admire each other terribly, but they think even higher of me myself.

6. Sam himself will give us a lift to the airport.

7. I declare: y'all's new pickup truck is just about as cute as a bug!

8. He up and made himself a mess of greens.

9. They helped themselves to a third dessert.

10. She gave him her hand, and they promised one another eternal love until death did them part.

(B) Write an original sentence containing the pronoun that the description refers to.

1. 2.sg., subject

2. 3.pl., reflexive

3. reciprocal

4. 1.pl., object

5. 1.sg., reflexive

6. 2.pl., object

7. 3.sg. feminine, subject

8. 2.sg. possessive determiner

9. 2.sg. possessive pronoun

10. 3.pl. possessive pronoun

(C) Write three original sentences containing reflexive pronouns.

1.

2.

3.

(D) Write three original sentences containing reciprocals.

1.

2.

3.

(E) Each of the following sentences contains something that is either stigmatized or ungrammatical. Find that something, explain why it is ungrammatical or (from the standpoint of prescriptive grammar) stigmatized and then correct it.

1. Him and me was late that day.

2. He would have given some to you and I if he'd wanted to.

3. Marco told me that Luigi saw each other in the mirror.

4. They asked himself what they had done wrong.

5. This one's yours and that one's mines.

6. The animal tried to extract it's paw from the trap.

(F) Explain the difference in **form and meaning** between each of the two sentences in the following pairs.

    1.a. I woke up at six.
       b. I woke him up at six.

    2.a. Sue said Sam saw her swim.
       b. Sue said Sam saw her swim suit.

(G) In what way is the following sentence potentially ambiguous? "Mary was telling me that Helga wanted to leave when she got sick."

Demonstratives

English has only four **demonstratives,** which can function as either **determiners** or as **pronouns:**

ENGLISH DEMONSTRATIVES

	singular	plural
near to speaker	this	these
near to hearer/ near to neither hearer nor speaker	that	those

These words function as determiners in the sense that they can constitute the first element in a noun phrase:

$$\text{I want} \begin{bmatrix} \text{the} \\ \text{a} \\ \text{this} \\ \text{that} \end{bmatrix} \text{horse.}$$

This/these/that/those are called **demonstratives** because they convey a high degree of specificity and distinctiveness in pointing out ("demonstrating") a referent; thus compare #1, 2, and 3 below:

1. I want an apple.
2. I want the apple.
3. I want this apple [as opposed to that apple or some other apple].

The **"near to speaker/near to hearer"** distinction enables us to differentiate between sentences such as the following:

4. I want these apples.
5. I want those apples.

In #4, the apples are assumed to be closer to the person speaking than to the person spoken to, whereas in #5 the apples are either closer to the listener than to the speaker or they are distant from the speaker and the listener alike.

So far, all the demonstratives we have exemplified have functioned as determiners that are accompanied by nouns in noun phrases. However, if the noun phrase's noun is deleted, one of two things can happen:

—the deleted noun is replaced by the indefinite pronoun <u>one</u> as in the following:

	1. I want that <u>apple</u> over there.
delete and replace	2. I want that <u>one</u> over there.

—the deleted noun is not replaced:

	3. I like <u>these</u> cats better than <u>those</u> cats.
delete only	4. I like <u>these</u> better than <u>those</u>.

In the case of sentence #2, the demonstrative remains a **determiner** (because it still precedes a slot that is filled—in this instance with the indefinite pronoun one). In the case of sentence #4, the demonstrative now functions as a **pronoun** because it is the sole component in its noun phrase, given the fact that the noun that followed it in #3 has been deleted, and nothing has taken that noun's place.

Indefinite Pronouns, Impersonal Pronouns

Like personal pronouns (pp. 179–83), **indefinite pronouns** are divided into two categories: those which bear antecedents, and those which do not have them. Thus:

<u>**ANTECEDENT-BEARING INDEFINITE PRONOUNS:**</u>

one

<u>**ANTECEDENT-LESS INDEFINITE PRONOUNS:**</u>

some { body
one
thing
where

any { body
one
thing
where

The fact that <u>one</u> has an antecedent is proven in sentence #1:

1. I like this <u>house</u> better than the other <u>one</u>.
    [Here, <u>one</u> refers back to <u>house</u>.]
2. Isn't Sam the <u>one</u> I met last year at the bris?
    [Here <u>one</u> is co-referential to <u>Sam</u>.]

Note that the word one is ambiguous as to its part of speech: in some contexts it is an **indefinite pronoun** and in other contexts it is an **impersonal pronoun** (while in yet other contexts it is a numeral, as in "One plus four equals five"). Here are several examples of one as an **impersonal pronoun**:

1. One lives and learns.
2. One does the best one can.
3. One must cut one's grass when it grows too tall.
4. One should attempt to live without drugs.

One as impersonal pronoun is understood to mean 'any person in general' without specifying which. Since no particular person is specified, the pronoun is impersonal, i.e., 'without person'. The impersonal one has no antecedent noun, whereas the antecedent-bearing indefinite one does. That is an important difference between the two. Another important difference is that impersonal one often functions as a subject and stands alone in its noun phrase, while indefinite one functions as readily as an object as it does as a subject, and usually does **not** stand alone in its noun phrase. Compare:

1. [impersonal as subject]
   One often learns things the hard way.
2. [indefinite as subject]
   This man drives a cab and that one drives a limo.

The eight antecedent-less indefinite pronouns are all compounds involving some or any. The difference between the two sets is semantic; thus anything denotes 'no limitation', whereas some sort of limitation is implied in something. Compare:

1. I'll buy you anything you want. [no limitation]
2. I'll buy you something you want. [some limitation]

We label the eight some-/any-indefinite pronouns **antecedent-less** because they do not conform to the patterns that have been established by the antecedent-bearing indefinite one; thus:

3. I like this house better than the other one.
4. *I like this house better than the other something.
5. *I like this house better than the something.
6. *I like this house better than the other anything.
   (etc.)

Relative Pronouns

A relative pronoun refers or relates back to an antecedent noun phrase that appears earlier in a sentence; example:

1. I bought a beagle hound <u>that</u> didn't bark.
antecedent	**rela-**
noun phrase	**tive**
	pronoun

2. She knows of a hospital <u>where</u> they give away drugs.
antecedent	**rela-**
noun phrase	**tive**
	pronoun

Relative pronouns typically initiate **relative clauses**, which, as clauses, would contain their own subject and verb if they were separated from the main sentence:

I bought a beagle hound. The beagle hound didn't bark.
repeated subject

I bought a beagle hound   t h a t   didn't bark.
relative pronoun
replacing the
repeated subject

Relative clauses will be discussed at greater length in ch. 6. For the moment it is enough to know which pronouns can function as relatives. They are:

that:	I know a man that poisoned his hamster.
<u>when:</u>	There will come a time when such crimes are punished
<u>where:</u>	She knows a place where we can be alone.
<u>which:</u>	I need a car which gets 100 miles to the gallon.
<u>who:</u>	We need a principal who can stand up to the gangs.
<u>whom:</u>	I once knew a man whom I admired greatly.
<u>whose:</u>	I knew a bartender whose wife was a famous chemist.
<u>why:</u>	I know the reason why you said it.

In stigmatized usage, <u>what</u> also functions as a relative pronoun, e.g., "Him 'n' me knows dis guy <u>what</u> done his wife in." Prescriptive English, however, never allows <u>what</u> to function as a relative pronoun.

The word <u>that</u> needs to be paid a bit more attention at this point. We have already seen that <u>that</u> can readily function as a **demonstrative,** and we have just examined the that that is used as a relative pronoun. However there is a third high-frequency usage of that—as something called a **complementizing conjunction** which we will not go into in any depth until ch. 8; for the moment it will suffice to know that any that that is neither a demonstrative nor a relative pronoun is a **comp-con**. A comp-con basically serves to join one detachable sentence to another in a subordinate compound sentence such as the following:

"I know that he is rich."

(Detachable sentence # 1: "I know [something].")
                            S   V   O

(Detachable sentence # 2: "He is rich.")
                            S V adjective

Interrogative Pronouns

Usable as **question words** at the beginning of questions are all the relative pronouns that begin with wh plus two others: how and what. These are the "wh words," which we illustrate below:

what:	What do you do for a living?
when:	When does the next flight depart?
where:	Where oh where did my little dog go?
which:	Which witch traded in her broomstick for a Lear jet?
who:	Who knows that The Shadow knows?
whom:	To whom am I speaking?
whose:	Whose car is this?
why:	Why do you do the things you do?
how:	How many times must I tell you that?

The syntax of the different question types involving interrogative pronouns has already been dealt with in ch. 3.

"Pro-Words": Pronoun-like Words for Sentences, Phrases, Adjectives, and Adverbs

These forms refer back to antecedent entities that are **not** nouns or noun phrases; that is why these forms are called pro-**words** and not pro-"nouns." The entity referred to can be a complete **sentence**:

1. Lulu said <u>she was going to die</u>. I told her I really
                complete sentence
didn't think <u>so</u>.
       pro-word

2. Miguel insisted <u>he would never fall in love again</u>, to
                   complete sentence
which I answered that I just couldn't believe <u>it</u>.
                                 pro-word

Or it can be an entire **verb phrase**:

3. Kowalczyk <u>climbed the Sears Tower</u> before Rydz did <u>so</u>.
       verb phrase   **pro-word**

It can be an **adjective**:

4. The Cookie Monster isn't really <u>despicable</u>; he just
                         adjective

seems <u>so</u>.
    pro-word

Or an **adverb**:

5. Vincent always does his work <u>carefully</u>; by working <u>thus</u>,
                    adverb   **pro-word**
he manages to achieve perfection.

The word <u>there</u> can function as a prepositional phrase pro-word (in which the prepositional phrase performs an adverbial function):

6. Sally was playing <u>in the attic</u> and left all her toys <u>there</u>.

The following items, then, can function as **pro-words**:

it
so
there
thus

(A) Underline and describe all **demonstratives** (whether **determiners** or **pronouns**), all **impersonal pronouns,** all **indefinite pronouns** (whether **antecedent-bearing** or **antecedent-less**), all **relative pronouns,** all **interrogative pronouns,** and all **pro-words** in the following sentences.

1. That car that you had last year was a lot more economical than this one.

2. I know a woman who takes in boarders that cannot pay.

3. How good are these?

4. Someone once asked me where I was from.

5. One often gets into trouble, so it's obvious that one can never be too careful.

6. Be careful with that one. It breaks easily.

7. Won't anybody out there do something to mend a broken heart?

8. I bought this bracelet at Tiffany's and then I left it there.

9. These new cars look shiny and those old ones look weather-beaten.

10. That man arrived long after the hour when the trains stop.

11. I knew that I was going to rob him, and I told him so.

12. Which witch bewitched this one? She looks terrible!

13. Who knows what will happen next?

14. Does anyone know what time it is?

15. Alice is a superb violinist and she has been one since age 12.

16. She sold me these, not those; I want my money back, and I have already told her so.

(B) Write original sentences which use the underlined words as the parts of speech indicated.

1. <u>anyone</u> as an antecedent-less indefinite pronoun

2. <u>what</u> as an interrogative pronoun

3. <u>that</u> as a relative pronoun

4. <u>so</u> as a pro-word

5. <u>those</u> as a demonstrative pronoun

6. <u>one</u> as an antecedent-bearing indefinite pronoun

7. <u>this</u> as a demonstrative pronoun

8. <u>there</u> as a pro-word

9. <u>when</u> as a relative pronoun

10. <u>something</u> as an antecedent-less indefinite pronoun

11. <u>which</u> as an interrogative pronoun

12. <u>which</u> as a relative pronoun

13. <u>that</u> as a demonstrative determiner

14. <u>that</u> as a demonstrative pronoun

6

ADJECTIVES AND RELATIVE CLAUSES

Attributive and Predicate Adjectives: Identification and Syntax

There are two positions in which an English adjective may appear: **before or after the noun it modifies**—the **attributive** position—or **after a verb**—the **predicate** position. Examples:

ATTRIBUTIVE

1.1 before the modified noun (the **pre-nominal** position)

  a. a big elephant
  b. the old computer
  c. some pretty women
  d. a poor little old green metal chair

1.2 after the modified noun (the **post-nominal** position)

  a. a woman big with child
  b. a course open to all students
  c. a driver asleep at the wheel

PREDICATE

2.a. the elephant is big
  b. some men were sick
  c. the women look pretty
  d. the dead roadrunner smells putrid
  e. the computer only seems old

While one of the most typical characteristics of English attributive adjectives is that they appear in the pre-nominal position, many attributive adjectives can appear post-nominally as well (thus big in nos. 1.1.a and 1.2.a. above), and a few appear only post-nominally (thus asleep in 1.2.c.; cf. the ungrammatical *"an asleep driver"). However, the expected or "unmarked" position for English adjectives is the pre-nominal attributive position. If an adjective appears in the post-nominal position, then that adjective will have formed part originally (or is assumed to have the potential to form part) of a **restrictive relative clause** that has undergone a transformation deleting the relative pronoun and the verb. (The deleted verb will have been a **copula** [be] or a copula-like verb [seem, appear, look].) Hence the following samples, which can be said to result from deletions such as these:

—a course [that is] open to all students
> **deletable**

—a driver [who was] asleep at the wheel
> **deletable**

—a feather [which looks] ruffled beyond belief
> **deletable**

—a decade [that seemed] lovely to remember
> **deletable**

(See this chapter's section on relative clauses for more information about relative clauses in general and the deletion of the relative pronouns that head them up.)

.   In the main, any attributive adjective, whether pre- or post-nominal, can be viewed as derived ultimately from a relative clause containing be plus the adjective itself. Thus note the following sentences:

The old man [= 'the man {who is} old'] lived to be 99.

Give me two and a half pieces of used bubblegum [= 'gum {that has been} used'].

EXERCISE 6.1

(A) Each of the following words is normally an adjective or can be used as one. Tell whether each can appear as a pre-nominal attributive only, as a post-nominal attributive only, as a predicate only, as all three of these, or as any two of them. Then use each adjective in one original sentence for each of the possibilities allowed.

    1. gray

    2. awake

    3. main

    4. medical

    5. former

    6. only

    7. extravagant

8. galore

9. daily

10. sleepy

11. responsible

12. stupid

13. innocent

14. total

15. Irish

(B) Locate the adjectives and then describe each one as prenominal attributive, post-nominal attributive, or predicate.

1. Jennifer bought a dripping taco at the Taco Tienda.

2. Send me the severed head of that brash young idealistic prophet.

3. Sam only appears exhausted after playing a full round of golf.

4. Julie rubbed expensive French ointment on tired fingers aching to the bone.

5. Sally is the recently appointed editor of a prestigious journal.

6. A sizzling roast dripping with fat landed on the back seat of my father's ancient Hupmobile.

7. Any face covered with acne is ugly in the eyes of prejudiced beholders.

8. Richard and Steve invested heavily in pure-bred collies.

9. The landed immigrant breathed a sigh pregnant with meaning.

10. Grant was awarded a fellowship whose terms were generous to a fault.

11. My sweet little old slivovitz-drinking Slovenian grandmother came to the New World in 1923.

12. The twins seemed inseparable until one of them had a terrible accident.

The Syntax of Pre-Nominal Attributive Adjectives

The importance of establishing syntactic rules for different types of attributive adjectives is highlighted by the following ungrammatical phrases:

1. *a hot nice bath
2. *a wintry cold day
3. *the fat big man
4. *several red little schoolhouses
5. *an Italian blue small automobile

Over the years, linguists have come up with increasingly fine-tuned rules for ordering strings of pre-nominal attributive adjectives. What we present here is a simplification of those rules, one that is cognizant of the fact that sequences of more than three adjectives are quite unusual. (Thus a phrase such as "a beautiful little dented old white Dutch metal teapot" would be roundly criticized on stylistic grounds if written, and would require a major feat of memory to utter.) Here then are the simplified rules for ordering pre-nominal attributive adjectives. (Non-adjective noun-phrase components such as determiners and the noun itself are enclosed in brackets.)

THE ORDERING OF PRE-NOMINAL ATTRIBUTIVE ADJECTIVES

[1 {= the first word in the noun phrase}: the determiner]
   2:    the **opinion-expresser**, e.g., good, bad, wonderful, nice
   3:    the **measurer**, with **size first**, then **shape**, e.g., big,
           little; round, square
   4:    the **condition-** or **age-expresser**, e.g., sick; young
   5:    the **color**
   6:    the **origin** or **material**
[7 {– the last word in the noun phrase}: the noun]

While even this simplified ordering is complex, and does not lend itself to any generalized statement, the following rule of thumb does a reasonably good job of expressing the essence of pre-nominal attributive adjective syntax:

> **The more intrinsic the adjective is to the nature of the noun, the closer to the noun the adjective is.**

EXERCISE 6.2

(A) Correct the following sentences if necessary, and explain your correction by citing the rules for pre-nominal attributive adjective ordering.

1. She's a Japanese small beautiful woman.

2. I want a big fat Slobovian pig to take to market.

3. They got a long lovely short-haired dachshund as a present.

4. He sold me a green medium-sized sweater.

5. Many fine upstanding young boys were led to slaughter.

6. That was a French little nice restaurant you took me to.

7. She said she would give me a new big brand-spanking great Cadillac for my birthday.

8. I understand that the Angolan bronze ancient marvellous statue they brought back was stolen.

Adjectives and Adverbs: The Comparative and Superlative Forms

As we recall from chapter 1, one important way to tell whether an English word can function as an adjective is to run it through the base (equative) form / comparative form / superlative form test, thus:

BASE (equative)	COMPARATIVE ("-er")	SUPERLATIVE ("-est")
old	older	oldest
as	*aser	*asest

Old, then, is an adjective while as is not.

Not all bona fide adjectives will pass this simple morphological test, since a general rule of English morphology is that all adjectives of three syllables or more—and some adjectives of two syllables—preface the base form with the free morpheme more to create the comparative and with the free morpheme most to create the superlative: more enthusiastic, most enthusiastic, etc. (The bound morphemes -er and -est are attached as suffixes to all adjectives of one syllable and to certain types of bisyllabic adjectives; see immediately below for more information.)

The Morphology of Comparatives: When to Use more and When -er

Here is the simplified three-part rule:

(1) Use only the bound morpheme (-er with:

—all one-syllable bases (nice, sweet, sick, tall, etc.)
—those two-syllable bases which end in:

-y ≠ -ly (e.g., happy, lucky, lazy, crazy, etc.)
$\left.\begin{array}{l} \text{-}\underline{p} \\ \text{-}\underline{b} \\ \underline{t} \\ \underline{d} \end{array}\right]$ le (e.g., simple, humble, little, idle)

(2) Use **either -er or more** with **all other two-syllable bases**, in particular these:

-ly: friendly—either friendlier or more friendly
-ow: shallow—shallower/more shallow
-er: eager—eagerer/more eager
-some: handsome—handsomer/more handsome

(Miscellaneous:

quiet: quieter/more quiet
stupid: stupider/more stupid)

It should be noted that in general, the two-syllable bases described here in paragraph 2 prefer to form their comparatives with <u>more</u> rather than with -<u>er</u>, so a good rule to go by is: when in doubt, opt for <u>more</u>.

(3) use ONLY <u>more</u> with all bases of three or more syllables:
conspicuous: more conspicuous
respectful: more respectful
insolent: more insolent
etc., etc.
(Note that if a two-syllable base takes -<u>er</u> alone, any derivation which converts the two syllables to three will not delete -<u>er</u>:
happy: happier
unhappy: unhappier.)

Six base forms take irregular comparative forms, i.e., forms whose comparatives use neither -<u>er</u> nor <u>more</u>. The six are:

BASE FORM	COMPARATIVE
much	more
many	more
little	less (But note "the littler of the two," "the littlest angel," both of which refer solely to size.)
good	better
bad	worse
far	farther ("measurable linear distance")
	further ("non-linear distance") (Note: it is increasingly the case that the difficult-to-remember <u>farther/further</u> distinction is being resolved in favor of <u>further</u>.)

The Morphology of Superlatives: When to Use -<u>est</u> and When <u>most</u>

All the morphological classifications that apply to comparatives apply to superlatives as well. Thus:

BASE FORM	COMPARATIVE	SUPERLATIVE
(1) tall	taller	tallest
happy	happier	happiest
little	littler	littlest

(2) friendly	friendlier/
	  more friendly
		friendliest/
		  most friendly

quiet	quieter/more quiet	quietest/most quiet
(3) conspicuous	more conspicuous	most conspicuous
respectful	more respectful	most respectful
Irregulars:		
much	more	most
many	more	most
little	less	least
good	better	best
bad	worse	worst
far	farther/further	farthest/furthest

Equatives, Comparatives, Superlatives: Construction and Meaning

First we must define some terms:

An **equative construction** typically states that A and B **are equal** when it comes to being, doing, or having X:

1. I have as much money as you do.
2. There are as many people in Albuquerque as there are in Tucson.
3. I work as hard as he does.

A **comparative construction** typically indicates that A has, is, or does **more than** B:

4. I have more money than you do.
5. There are more people in Fort Dodge than there are in Grundy Center.
6. I work harder than he does.

A **superlative construction** attributes to A the top quality or the bottom quality on a scale:

7. I have the most money in town.
8. Mexico D.F. is the largest city in the world.
9. I work hardest of all.
10. Piggy is the fattest kid in the whole third grade.
11. Old Professor Fidgit owns the most books on Ancient Aramaic of anyone in his profession.

The superlative deals in absolutes. While it is often used to compare one entity to more than two ("That cow is the most bovine animal in the whole herd!"), a superlative construction can also be used to compare just two entities for X, provided that the X-ness in question is being viewed as measurable by some sort of absolute standard; thus "Rockefeller and Onassis—which one of them was the richest [millionaire of all]?" (Using the superlative to compare just two entities is especially typical of colloquial language and is still condemned by some prescriptivists.)

Adjectives and adverbs enter directly into equative, comparative and superlative constructions; nouns (and verbs) enter into them in a more peripheral way. (Nouns can be modified by quantifiers such as many, much, few, little, several, a lot of, etc., thereby enabling them to participate in comparative and superlative constructions. Verbs in verb phrases can be followed by an expression of quantity, traditionally called an adverbial of extent or degree, e.g., "They jog a little every morning," "Hillary used to bake cookies a lot," "Laura bakes more than she does," etc.) Here is a list of all twelve possibilities—each of the three constructions involving each of the four parts of speech. This list also provides occasional important comments on any relationship between a particular construction's form and the special or unexpected meaning it may have.

EQUATIVE/COMPARATIVE/SUPERLATIVE CONSTRUCTIONS

EQUATIVE STRUCTURES   . . . as ———— as . . .
AND MEANINGS:

adjective	1. He's as old as you (are).
adverb	2. He eats as fast as you (do).
noun	3. He has as many books as you (do).
verb	4. He studies as much as you (do).

(Note: elements between parentheses are optional. The deletion of the verb creates a "reduced" clause.)

COMPARATIVE STRUCTURES   . . . ——er than . . .
AND MEANINGS: . . . more —— than . . . //
                             . . . fewer ———— than . . .
                             . . . less ———— than . . .

adjective	5. He's older than you (are).
adverb	6. He's not as young as you (are).

Note that while the **structure** of #6 is **equative**, the **meaning** is **comparative**. Sentence 6 demonstrates that when EQUATIVE structures are NEGATED—**not** as young as you—their MEANING becomes COMPARATIVE; one can make an analogy with the scales of justice, which when **not** balanced at the same level **cease** to dispense [equative] "equal justice". Here are two other examples of equative structures which produce comparative meanings because the structure's verb is negated by the addition of not:

—I don't like Mozart as much as you do.

　　[This means "You like Mozart more than I do."]

—He didn't have as many properties as you did.

　　[This means "You had more properties than he."]

adverb　　　7. He eats faster than you (do).

　　　　8. He doesn't eat as slowly as you (do).

　　　　　(Sentence #8 is another example of a negated equative construction producing a comparative meaning.)

noun　　　9. She has more money than you (do).

　　　　10. She has fewer properties than you (do).

　　　　11. Joan has less income than he (does).

verb　　　12. She studies more than you (do).

　　　　13. Slobovians work harder than Cherts (do).

SUPERLATIVE STRUCTURES
AND MEANINGS:

　　　　　. . . the ————(e)st of . . .

　　　　　. . . the least/most ———— of . . .

adjective　　14. She's the oldest of all.

　　　　15. She's the most paranoid of all.

adverb　　　16. He eats the fastest of all.

　　　　17. He eats faster than anyone.

Note that while the **structure** of #17 is **comparative**, #17's **meaning** is **superlative** because of the presence in the sentence of the indefinite pronoun <u>anyone</u>, which expands the sentence's parameters to the point of de facto universality: "than anyone" taken literally could encompass the entire world! Sentence #17 then is an example of a comparative structure used to superlative effect. Here are two more examples of the same thing:

—It rained harder than anything I had ever seen.

—Gordon is fatter than anyone we have ever met.

　　　　18. No one eats faster than he (does).

　　　　　(This comparative structure produces superlative meaning because of the presence of the negative indefinite pronoun <u>no one</u>.)

　　　　19. No one eats as fast as she (does).

　　　　　(This equative structure produces superlative meaning because of the presence of the negative indefinite pronoun <u>no one</u>.)

noun　　　20. She has the most books of anyone ([that] I know).

　　　　21. She has more books than anyone ([that] I know).

　　　　　(This comparative structure produces superlative meaning because of the presence of <u>anyone</u>.)

　　　　22. No one has as many books as she (does).

　　　　　(Equative structure, superlative meaning.)

verb　　　23. He studies the most of anyone ([that] I know).

　　　　24. He studies more than anyone ([that] I know).

Equatives with Comparative Meanings. Equatives and Comparatives with Superlative Meanings

By now it is clear that EQUATIVES take on COMPARATIVE meanings under the following condition:

—when the verb is negated by the addition of <u>not</u>:
   a. He's not as young as you (are).
   b. He doesn't eat as slowly as you (do).

By now it is also clear that both EQUATIVE and COMPARATIVE constructions take on SUPERLATIVE meanings under the following conditions:

—the subject of the sentence is the negative indefinite pronoun <u>no one</u>:
   c. No one studies as much as she does.
   d. No one studies more than she does.
—the entity which the subject is being compared to is the indefinite pronoun <u>any one</u>:
   e. Quincy studies more than anyone.
   f. Quincy has more money than anyone.

This shows, then, that it is important to pay attention to the **meaning** as well as to the **construction** when determining the equative, comparative, or superlative message the sentence is trying to get across.

EXERCISE 6.3

(A) Provide the comparative and the superlative forms for each of the following equatives.

1. dumb

2. ravishing

3. tricky

4. subtle

5. devastated

6. repentant

7. slow

8. valid

9. lovely

10. negotiable

11. urgent

12. luscious

13. sadistic

14. mobile

15. gross

16. cannibalistic

(B) Identify each of the following sentences as to (1) **construction** and (2) **equative, comparative, or superlative meaning.**

1. I have as many friends as Joe.

2. Carol is the most prolific writer of her generation.

3. She has written more successful fiction than anybody.

4. Sue is not as pretty as you are, but she certainly is bright.

5. Mirror, mirror on the wall, who's the fairest of them all?

6. Dr. Finkel sees four fewer patients than Dr. Funkel.

7. I wouldn't dance as slowly as you if I didn't have this cast on my leg.

8. Not one single Boy Scout earned as many merit badges as Percival did.

9. Some people say that prostitution is the oldest profession in the world.

10. I work harder than Tom, Rick, or Harriet.

11. The anteater scarfs down ants faster than any other animal.

   12. No one plays bridge as well as my Great-Aunt Agatha.

(C) Write one original sentence corresponding to each of the following descriptions.

   1. superlative construction, superlative meaning; noun

   2. equative construction, superlative meaning; noun

   3. comparative construction, comparative meaning; adjective

   4. comparative construction, superlative meaning; verb

   5. equative construction, equative meaning; adverb

   6. comparative construction, comparative meaning; adverb

   7. superlative construction, superlative meaning; adjective

8. equative construction, equative meaning; noun

9. comparative construction, superlative meaning; adverb

10. comparative construction, comparative meaning; noun

Relative Clauses. Relative Pronouns and Their Antecedents

It will be recalled from chapter 5 that there are seven relative pronouns—that, when, where, which, who/whom, whose, and why—[5] and that a relative pronoun refers or "relates" to an antecedent noun phrase appearing early in the sentence.

What types of antecedents can relative pronouns take? Semantic considerations play a large role in determining this. For example, when's antecedent must refer to something definable in terms of time ("I can remember the day when you were born"), and why's antecedent must have to do with some sort of explanation or justification ("Let me tell you the reason why I've changed my mind"). The following table gives the semantic parameters of the remaining relative pronouns:

who/whom:
+human (i.e., can only take a human antecedent)
Melanie is a woman who(m) I am very fond of.
*Bourbon is a drink who(m) I am very fond of.

whose:
+/−human (the antecedent is usually human, but it can be non-human as well)
+human:
  Scarlet was a woman whose hoopskirt never stopped twirling.
−human:
  West Texas crude is the oil whose value sets the mark for the industry.

that:
+/−human (but that can never be used as the object of a preposition):
  The man that I saw in the store said hello.
  The car that sat in the driveway was for sale.
  *The car on that the cat sat was old and dirty.

which:
typically [−human], and can be used as the object of a preposition:
  The car which sat in the driveway was for sale.
  The car on which the cat sat was dirty.
  *The man which I saw in the store said hello.
  (But note: ?"The people which I wanted to see weren't there." It appears that if the + human antecedent is collective, which may possibly be used to refer to it. Native informants differ as to the acceptability of a sentence like "The people which I wanted to see . . .")

Since who/whom, whose, and that can all take human antecedents, how do we know which one to use, and when? Right away we can establish some rather narrow parameters for whose, as it is used exclusively as a possessive, and sentences containing it can be viewed as combinations or mergers such as the following:

> Fido is a dog.
> Fido's bone is buried.
>
> **possessive**
> **(genitive)**
> Fido is a dog/Fido's bone is buried. →→→
> w h o s e
> Fido is a dog whose bone is buried.

That leaves who/whom and that, neither of which is ever possessive. Here then are the differences between who/whom and that:

(1) that and who never function as an object of a preposition. Only whom can do so. Examples:

1. I would like you to meet the woman to whom I am engaged.
2. *I would like you to meet the woman to that I am engaged.
3. *I would like you to meet the woman to who I am engaged.

(2) Who, whom, and that are usable in all other pronominal functions, but there is a style or register difference between them: who/whom are perceived as being more elegant, and that is perceived as more colloquial. For example:

3. The man who I made the offer to has accepted.
4. The man whom I made the offer to has accepted.
5. The man that I made the offer to has accepted.

When to Use **Who** and When to Use **Whom**

The -m-form—whom—**must be used if the preceding word is its governing preposition.** Note the following:

6. Who are you speaking to?
7. Whom are you speaking to?
8. To whom are you speaking?
9. *To who are you speaking?

If to or another preposition precedes the relative pronoun, only the -m form is grammatical. But if there is no preceding word or if the preceding word is not a preposition, then either <u>who</u> or <u>whom</u> can be used as an object-case relative pronoun.

Deleting Relative Pronouns: The Creation of Gaps

In many environments the relative pronoun can be deleted. Doing so creates a **gap**, or empty space, which can always be filled again by reinserting the deleted relative pronoun. Here are some examples; the deletable relative pronoun appears between brackets.

1. The man [that] I made the offer to has accepted.
2. The elephant [which] I saw yesterday died this morning.
3. She told the girl [who(m)] you gave the money to a secret.
4. The manager [that] you spoke about is their friend.

Relative pronoun gaps can only be created if the relative pronoun functions as an object in its relative clause. Such gaps cannot be created if the relative pronoun functions as the **subject** of its relative clause (or if the relative pronoun is immediately preceded by the preposition that governs it). Consider these examples:

5. [RELATIVE PRONOUN AS DIRECT OBJECT IN ITS RELATIVE CLAUSE]

   The elephant [which] I saw yesterday died this morning.

When **deconstructed** into its constituent elements, this compound sentence produces these two simple sentences:

   a. **[main clause]** The elephant died this morning.
   b. **[relative clause]** I saw the elephant yesterday.

Here is the process by which these two deconstructed sentences are transformed or "merged back" into a compound sentence:

1. The elephant / I saw <u>the elephant</u> yesterday / died this morning.
   direct object
2. The elephant / I saw w h i c h   yesterday / died this morning.
3. The elephant /w h i c h I saw   yesterday / died this morning.
   → **The elephant which I saw yesterday died this morning.**

The process works like this: (a) you establish the fact that in sentence # 1 the first elephant and the second elephant "are the same elephant," i.e., they are co-referential, or **equivalent**; (b) you replace the elephant of the relative clause with its corresponding relative pronoun; and (c) you move the relative pronoun to the beginning of the relative clause.

6. [RELATIVE PRONOUN AS THE SUBJECT OF ITS RELATIVE CLAUSE]

The goat that chewed the tin can is my pet.

Since the relative pronoun that is the **subject** of its relative clause, that cannot be deleted, and no gap can be created. Note the following ungrammatical sentence:[6]

*The goat chewed the tin can is my pet.

Let us now **deconstruct** sentence #6 to prove that that functions as the subject of its relative clause:

1. The goat / the goat chewed the tin can / is my pet.
                    subject verb   direct object
2. The goat / that chewed the tin can / is my pet.
    →→ **The goat that chewed the tin can is my pet.**

The above two examples merely represent the start of our analysis, since there are a total of 20 types of relative clauses all told. The following chart lists all 20 types and gives examples of each. First note the term **antecedent (pro)noun**; this term refers to the **main-clause noun or pronoun which is the antecedent of the relative pronoun** in the relative clause. (The main clause starts at the beginning of the sentence; the relative clause appears in the middle or at the end.) Now note the term **relativized noun;** it is the noun in the relative clause that ends up being replaced by the relative pronoun there. Also note that all relative pronouns which can be gapped are written between parentheses. Here is an example:

She knows the man (that) you discussed.
S h e   knows   t h e m a n / you discussed t h e m a n.
head   direct object—   direct object
(pro)noun   relativized noun
She   knows   t h e m a n   you discussed   t h a t
She   knows   t h e m a n   t h a t you discussed
→→ She knows the man that you discussed.

RELATIVE CLAUSE STRUCTURES—THE 20 TYPES AND EXAMPLES

Function of the antecedent (pro)noun in its main clause	Function of the relative pronoun in its relative clause

subject

SUBJECT:

1. The man who sings Wagner is their friend.
    The man / the man sings Wagner / is their friend

DIRECT OBJECT:

2. She knows the man who sings Wagner.
    She knows the man / the man sings Wagner

INDIRECT OBJECT:

3. We gave the singer who broke the glass a standing ovation.
    We gave the singer / the singer broke the glass / a standing ovation
also: We gave a standing ovation to the singer who broke the glass.
    We gave a standing ovation to the singer / the singer broke the glass

OBJECT OF A PREPOSITION:

4. I'm talking with the woman who sings Wagner.
    I'm talking with the woman / the woman sings Wagner

PREDICATE NOUN:

5. Giorgio is the singer who hates Wagner.
    Giorgio is the singer / the singer hates Wagner

direct object

SUBJECT:

1. The man (who) you met is their friend.
    The man / you met the man / is their friend

DIRECT OBJECT:

2. She knows the man (who) you discussed.
    She knows the man / you discussed the man

INDIRECT OBJECT:

3.   We sent the singer (who) Brunhilde saw a helmet.
        We sent the singer / Brunhilde saw the singer / a helmet
also: We sent a helmet to the singer (who) Brunhilde saw.
        We sent a helmet to the singer / Brunhilde saw the singer

OBJECT OF A PREPOSITION:

4.   I'm talking with the woman (who) you met.
        I'm talking with the woman / you met the woman

PREDICATE NOUN:

5.   Wagner is the composer (who) Giorgio hates.
        Wagner is the composer / Giorgio hates the composer

indirect object

SUBJECT:

1.   The man (who) I gave the helmet to is their friend.
        The man / I gave the helmet to the man / is their friend
also: The man to whom I gave the helmet is their friend.
        The man / I gave the helmet to the man / is their friend

DIRECT OBJECT:

2.   I mentioned the man (who) you gave the helmet to.
        I mentioned the man / you gave the helmet to the man

INDIRECT OBJECT:

3.   He told the singer (who) you gave the helmet to a secret.
        He told the singer / you gave the helmet to the singer / a secret
also: He told the singer to whom you gave the helmet a secret.
        He told the singer / you gave the helmet to the singer / a secret
also: He told a secret to the singer to whom you gave the helmet.
        He told a secret to the singer / you gave the helmet to the singer

OBJECT OF A PREPOSITION:

4.   I'm talking with the woman (who) I gave the helmet to.
        I'm talking with the woman / I gave the helmet to the woman
also: I'm talking with the woman to whom I gave the helmet.
        I'm talking with the woman / I gave the helmet to the woman

PREDICATE NOUN:

5.   Giorgio is the singer (who) I gave the helmet to.
        Giorgio is the singer / I gave the helmet to the singer
also: Giorgio is the singer to whom I gave the helmet.
        Giorgio is the singer / I gave the helmet to the singer

object of a preposition

SUBJECT:

1.   The man about whom you spoke is their friend.
       The man / you spoke about the man / is their friend

also: The man (who) you spoke about is their friend.
       The man / you spoke about the man / is their friend

DIRECT OBJECT:

2.   I know the man about whom you spoke.
       I know the man / you spoke about the man

also: I know the man (who) you spoke about.
       I know the man / you spoke about the man

INDIRECT OBJECT:

3.   We gave the singer about whom you were talking the helmet.
       We gave the singer / you were talking about the singer / the helmet

also: We gave the helmet to the singer about whom you were talking.
       We gave the helmet to the singer / you were talking about the singer

also: We gave the singer (who) you were talking about the helmet.
       We gave the singer / you were talking about the singer / the helmet

also: We gave the helmet to the singer (who) you were talking about.
       We gave the helmet to the singer / you were talking about the singer

OBJECT OF A PREPOSITION:

4.   I'm talking with the woman about whom you spoke.
       I'm talking with the woman / you spoke about the woman

also: I'm talking with the woman (who) you spoke about.
       I'm talking with the woman / you spoke about the woman

PREDICATE NOUN:

5.   Giorgio is the singer with whom I'm talking.
       Giorgio is the singer / I'm talking with the singer

also: Giorgio is the singer (who) I'm talking with.
       Giorgio is the singer / I'm talking with the singer

The Relativization of the Possessive Determiner <u>whose</u>

Any one of the 20 structures in the chart we have just presented can substitute a relative clause beginning with <u>whose</u> for the relative clause it already contains. The relative <u>whose</u> is a determiner that indicates possession. Here is an example:

1. She knows the man who you discussed.
→ → → 2. She knows the man <u>whose father</u> you discussed.

What follows is the process by which we reach sentence # 2:

She knows the man. + You discussed <u>the man's father</u>.
You discussed <u>whose father</u>
<u>whose father</u> you discussed
→ → → She knows the man <u>whose father</u> you discussed.

EXERCISE 6.4

(A) Underline all the **relative pronouns**.

Indicate their **antecedents**.

Then specify the **case** of relative pronouns and antecedents alike—subject, direct object, indirect object, object of preposition, or predicate noun.

Finally, **deconstruct** the relativized sentence into its two component sentences: main clause and relative clause.

1. I found the girl who had been to Siberia.

2. He knows the librarian who Sandy threw a book at.

3. They wanted to see the dog that you had found.

4. The air which we breathe is full of dust.

5. My wife gave the old lady who you had told me about the money.

6. Last night I finally understood the theory that we had studied.

7. War and Peace is the novel that I'm reading right now.

8. The author to whom you spoke is none other than Philip Roth himself.

9. I told the little girl that the old man gave the candy to not to cry.

10. I want to know the issue that we will be discussing today.

11. The cat that escaped from the basement just had kittens.

12. The question that concerns us today is: should the beggar to whom you gave your life's savings return them?

13. We sold the gun to the assassin who paid the highest price.

14. That <u>that</u> that that <u>that</u> modifies is misplaced in that phrase.

(B) Find the gaps and reinstate the deleted relative pronouns. (In some instances, no relative pronouns have been deleted.)

    1. The dog I gave the bone to wagged its tail.

    2. She wants her to find the thief she was talking about.

    3. The con-artist who you saw cheat the poor old man has vanished into thin air.

    4. I found the money the thief the police captured had hidden.

5. I know the basement he hid it in and the exact minute he hid it.

6. The issue you are referring to has already been dealt with.

7. We gave the boy who won the race a silver dollar.

8. The ghastly ghost I lent my body to said subsequently that I was the man he had picked for further nocturnal escapades.

(C) Each of the following sentences contains at least one grammar mistake. Correct it, then explain why you have done so, citing rules.

1. *The boss to that I am supposed to report is sick today.

2. *A woman whom I must speak has left the office.

3. *Where is the clerk to who I was told to give this message?

4. *There's the man what I want to see.

5. *Someone who's money I stole wants it back.

6. *Who's the little kid which says he's lost?

7. *I never did locate the loanshark I wanted to pay him back the money.

8. *He sold the diamonds to the smuggler whom was going to give them to his wife on her birthday.

9. *The man says he's president was arrested again for lewd behavior.

(D) **Identify** all relative clauses and then **deconstruct** the relativized sentences into their two component parts.

1. I will soon be talking with the young woman to whom I awarded the presidential scholarship.

2. He's currently writing to the prisoner you told me about.

3. The cat that ate the rat is fat.

4. She told the lawyer you hired a lie.

5. Connie is the student Tom talks about most.

6. They will send the boy they gave their address to a model airplane.

7. They will send a model airplane to the boy to whom they gave their address.

8. Sam is the math teacher who loves opera most.

9. You just saw the man who shot JFK.

10. He gave the rabid dog you were looking for a shot.

11. Bob is the newscaster I'm having an affair with.

Restrictive and Non-Restrictive Clauses

Compare the following two sentences:

1. The children who were in the cancer ward cried all night.
        restrictive clause
2. The children, who were in the cancer ward, cried all night.
        non-restrictive clause

The relative clause in #1 is termed **restrictive** because it restricts or limits its antecedent—the children—to one certain set of children only, and implicitly contrasts those children to all others. ("Children," then, are divisible in sentence #1 into two sets: those which were in the cancer ward, and those which were not.) The relative clause in # 2 is termed **non-restrictive** because it does **not** limit or restrict its antecedent; instead, the information about the cancer ward is after the fact, off-hand, ancillary, almost an afterthought.

Non-restrictive relative clauses are always set off by commas. Restrictive clauses never are.

Restrictive clauses occupy all the cases that are set forth in the "Relative Clause Structures" table presented on pp. 227–29. Non-restrictive clause relative pronouns appear to be limited to functioning as subjects. However, English frequently employs the relative pronoun which in three non-restrictive clause or phrase types as a **pro-word** and not as a pronoun (see ch. 5). Here are the three types:

(1) **adjective phrase:**
    Here, the relative pro-word (pro-adjective) shares co-referentiality with an adjective that appears in the sentence's main clause. Examples:

1. He's miserable, which I don't think you are.

    DECONSTRUCTION:
            He's miserable.
            I don't think you are miserable.
            I don't think you are which
            which I don't think you are
    →→→ He's miserable, which I don't think you are.)

2. The peasants' life is wretched, which yours certainly is not.

    DECONSTRUCTION:
            The peasants' life is wretched.
            Yours certainly is not wretched.
            Yours certainly is not which
            which yours certainly is not
    →→→ The peasants' life is wretched, which yours certainly is not.

(2) verb phase:

Here the "pro-verb" relativizing element (which) enjoys co-referentiality with the verb of the main clause. Examples:

1. Zack placed dozens of explicit ads in the personals column, which I could never do.

   DECONSTRUCTION:

   > Zack placed dozens of explicit ads in the personals column.
   > I could never place dozens of explicit ads in the personals column.
   > I could never which
   > which I could never do

   →→→ Zack placed dozens of explicit ads in the personals column, which I could never do.

2. She tried to sing, which I didn't.

   DECONSTRUCTION:

   > She tried to sing.
   > I didn't try to sing.
   > I didn't which
   > which I didn't

   →→→ She tried to sing, which I didn't.

(3) sentence clause:

The "pro-sentence" relative which is co-referential with the entire main clause of the sentence, as the following examples will show:

1. My brother got drunk and stayed out late last night, which angered my father.
   (Commentary: which refers neither to night nor brother nor got drunk nor stayed out late, but to a combination of all these elements together.)

   DECONSTRUCTION:

   > My brother got drunk and stayed out late last night.
   > That my brother got drunk and stayed out late last night angered my father.
   > Which angered my father
   > My brother got drunk and stayed out late last night, which angered my father.

2. Several large muddy dalmatians galloped through the cozy little tea room, <u>which</u> completely ruined the intimate tea party taking place there.

    DECONSTRUCTION:

    > Several large muddy dalmatians galloped . . .
    >
    > That several large muddy dalmatians galloped . . . com-<u>pletely ruined the intimate tea party</u> . . .
    >
    > <u>Which</u> completely ruined the intimate tea party . . .

EXERCISE 6.5

(A) Write three pairs of restrictive clause/non-restrictive clause sentences. Then explain the differences in meaning between each pair's sentences.

1. a.

   b.

2. a.

   b.

3. a.

   b.

(B) Tell whether the following non-restrictive-clause sentences contain **adjective-phrase** pro-forms, **verb-phrase** pro-forms, or **sentence-clause** pro-forms. Be sure to **identify** antecedents and pro-forms in every instance.

1. Tom regularly told everything, which was a source of constant delight for us all.

2. I am very happy, which my friends are too.

3. They are just tickled pink over the birth of their new baby girl, which we are as well.

4. The queen's consort has left her, which makes her very sad.

5. The baby screamed and screamed, which drove me crazy.

6. Bruce quickly climbed to the top of the mountain, which I didn't have the energy to attempt.

Present Participle Relative Pronoun Clauses.

Past Participle Relative Pronoun Clauses.

Both types of pronoun phrases involve the creation of a gap. In each instance, the gap is created at the head of the phrase by deleting (1) the relative pronoun itself, and (2) the tense-marked form of the verb be. What remains is the participle (present or past) and the LV. Here are several examples:

PRESENT PARTICIPLE R.P. CLAUSE:

1. The checks that were being cashed bore my signature.

ante-	rel.	tense-	pre-	LV
cedent	pron.	marked	sent	
noun		form	parti-	
		of BE	ciple	

relative pronoun clause:

deletion to create gap:

The checks being cashed bore my signature.

2. Take special precautions with prisoners who are undergoing punishment.

deletion to create gap:

Take special precautions with prisoners undergoing punishment.

3. All foreign debt extensions which are currently under consideration will be discussed tomorrow.

deletion to create gap:

All foreign debt extensions currently under consideration will be discussed tomorrow.

4. Any student who was smoking in the restroom would be expelled immediately.

deletion to create gap:

Any student smoking in the restroom would be expelled immediately.

PAST PARTICIPLE R.P. CLAUSE:

5. The child <u>who was killed by the stray bullet</u> was only four.

           <u>relative pronoun clause</u>

ante-	rel.	tense-	LV
cedent	pro.	marked	
noun		form	
		of <u>BE</u>	

deletion to create gap:

The child killed by the stray bullet was only four.

6. It's impossible to estimate the total amount of money <u>which is stolen by organized crime.</u>

deletion to create gap:

It's impossible to estimate the total amount of money stolen by organized crime.

7. The ship <u>that was sunk by torpedoes</u> now lies below.

deletion to create gap:

The ship sunk by torpedoes now lies below.

EXERCISE 6.6

(A) Reinstate the deleted relative pronouns and the tense-bearing <u>be</u> forms.

1. All dog owners recently bitten by their pets must report to the hospital immediately.

2. The six sick Sikhs soundly sleeping in the sanitarium suddenly sought safety Saturday.

3. Henry mastered four dead languages previously spoken in the eastern Mediterranean.

4. The man murdered by the Mafia managed to mail a message to his mother Monday morning from Miami.

5. I'll never forget those happy childhood scenes of kids playing hide and go seek on a warm summer's evening.

6. Now is the time for all good men bled dry by the tax department to rise up in outraged protest.

(B) Write four original pairs of sentences the second of which deletes the relative pronoun and the tense-marked be form but the first of which does not. Make sure that two of the pairs employ present participles and two of the pairs employ past.

1. a.

   b.

2. a.

   b.

3. a.

   b.

4. a.

   b.

7

ADVERBS.
IT AND THERE: REFERENTIALS AND
NON-REFERENTIALS. CLEFTS.

Adverbs

There are four major categories of adverbs, a part of speech which elementary textbooks typically define in a flawed and incomplete fashion as "words ending in -ly that modify verbs, adjectives, or other adverbs." (The problem with this definition is that not all words ending in -ly are adverbs—cf. the adjective ugly and not all adverbs end in -ly, e.g., tomorrow ['I will see him tomorrow'], hard ['I will work hard'], and soon ['The job will be done soon']. However, equating -ly with the category **adverb** is nonetheless a good starting point for a more sophisticated study of the adverb phenomenon, which we propose to offer here.)

The four major categories of adverbs are:

(1) **manner** adverbs (which typically modify verbs)

Manner adverbs always lend themselves to the following paraphrase or restatement:

"_____(VERB)_____ in an XXXX manner (or way, or sense)"

Here are several examples:

1. Casimir walked slowly up the hill.
   paraphrase: . . . walked in a slow manner
2. Gertrude happily cried herself to sleep.
   paraphrase: . . . cried in a happy manner
3. The sheep grazed in the meadow lazily.
   paraphrase: . . . grazed in a lazy manner
4. We literally ran out of gas.
   paraphrase: . . . ran out of gas in a literal (not a figurative) sense

251

(2) **gradational** adverbs (which typically modify adjectives or other adverbs)

> **Gradational adverbs** answer the question "to what degree of intensity?" The word <u>gradational</u> conjures up the image of a **degree** on a measuring scale. Consider the following sentences:
>
> 4. Anne-Marie is very happy.
>   **question:** To what degree is Anne-Marie happy: "extremely" happy, "slightly" happy, "sort of" happy, "very" happy . . .?
> 5. Jean-Pierre was somewhat glad to see us.
>   **question:** To what degree was Jean-Pierre glad to see us: to a "moderate" degree ('somewhat'), to an "extreme" degree ('tremendously') . . .?

Since gradational adverbs typically modify adjectives or other adverbs, another way to show whether a given adverb is gradational is to ask: does the clause in which it appears contain another adverb? an adjective? If so, then does the suspected gradational adverb make a "degree" statement about that adjective or other adverb?

(3) **standpoint** adverbs

> **Standpoint adverbs** typically modify adjectives, but differ from gradational adverbs as to the question they ask. While gradationals ask about degrees on a scale, standpoints speak in terms of the **perspective or standpoint from which something is viewed**. We use a **standpoint paraphrase** to prove that an adverb is or is not a standpoint adverb. Thus:

> 6. Your reasoning is logically impossible.
>   **paraphrase:**   Your reasoning is impossible from the standpoint of logic.
> 7. Quantum mathematics was viewed at first as theoretically unlikely.
>   **paraphrase:**   Quantum mathematics was viewed at first as unlikely from the standpoint of [mathematical] theory.

Let us now prove that a standpoint adverb is neither a manner adverb nor a gradational adverb:
standpoint adverb submitted to a MANNER paraphrase:
  *Your reasoning is impossible in a logical manner.

standpoint adverb submitted to a GRADATIONAL paraphrase:
—Your reasoning is logically impossible.
—To what degree [of intensity]?
—*To a logical degree.
(One cannot speak of something being impossible to a logical degree.)

(4) **sentence** adverbs

Sentence adverbs are like sentence-phrase pro-forms (ch. 5) in that they modify the entire sentence they form part of. To show that something is a **sentence adverb** we make use of a **sentence-adverb paraphrase,** which goes like this:
"It is _____X_____ that ..."

Here are some examples of sentence adverbs:
8. You clearly intend to get drunk tonight.

   paraphrase: "It is clear that you intend to get drunk tonight."

9. He has evidently had a hard time at work.

   paraphrase: "It is evident that he has had a hard time at work."

Note that none of the other adverbials' paraphrases or tests can apply to sentence adverbs:
MANNER: *You intend to get drunk tonight in a clear manner.
GRADATIONAL: "To what degree of intensity do you intend to get drunk?" — "*To a clear degree."
STANDPOINT: *You intend to get drunk tonight from the standpoint of clear/clarity/clearness.

Adverbs denoting time—a major category in English—are also **sentence adverbs,** as the following shows:
10. They arrived late.
    paraphrase: It was late when they arrived.
    (Cf. *They arrived in a late manner/*They arrived to a late degree of intensity/*They arrived from the standpoint of late/lateness.)
11. The plane will arrive at 5:15 p.m.
    paraphrase: It will be 5:15 p.m. when the plane arrives.

Adverbs denoting time always answer the question "When?" Other questions that adverbs typically answer are: "Where?" "To what degree?" "How?"

EXERCISE 7.1

(A) Classify each adverb or adverbial phrase as either **manner, gradational, standpoint,** or **sentence** and then **prove your classification through paraphrase or some other test.** (If an adverb lends itself to more than one classification, show how that is so.)

1. They are slightly ashamed of what they did.

2. The horses cantered lazily down the road.

3. Such a surgical procedure is medically risky.

4. He has always wanted to be able to run fast.

5. Monkeys obviously love bananas.

6. Monkeys love bananas obviously.

7. We had a totally fabulous time at your party.

8. They certainly like to drink, don't they?

9. We had planned on leaving yesterday, but something came up at the last minute.

10. English two-word verbs are syntactically complicated.

11. Rapidly careening downstream, the canoe slowly began to leak.

12. I'm just moderately tired after doing all this work.

13. Unfortunately every generation has its share of liars, cheats, and psychopaths.

14. We are going to leave now.

(B) Use each of the following adverbs in an original sentence and then classify the adverb as to its category.

1. happily

2. obviously

3. totally

4. somewhat

5. tomorrow

6. possessively

7. psychologically

8. radically

9. quickly

10. awfully

11. real

12. kind of

It as Referential, It as Non-Referential

Consider the word it in the following sentence:

1. Do you remember where I stored my suitcase? It might be in the attic, or it might have been left in the garage.

In this sentence, it clearly refers back to the singular object noun suitcase; = 1's it, then, is a typical 3.sg. direct object pronoun; it and suitcase are therefore co-referential; consequently, it enjoys **referential** status. Now compare sentence #1 and its usage of it to the following sentence's:

2. Do you really think we should go to the beach? It looks like it is going to rain.

In sentence #2, it is obviously not co-referential with beach, as the following proves:

3. *The beach looks like the beach is going to rain.

Nor can we claim that #2's it is some sort of sentence-level pro-form on the order of which, what, or the fact that as presented in chapter 6, since the following two sentences do not pattern alike at all:

4. [sentence-level pro-form:]
My brother got drunk and stayed out late is what really made my father mad.
5. [NOT a sentence-level pro-form:]
*Your really thinking we should go to the beach is what looks like it is going to rain.

Where, then, does the it of sentence #2 come from if it cannot constitute a co-referential copy of some anterior antecedent? There are several explanations, which we will examine shortly; but one of the best explanations of the origin and presence of this it goes as follows: **EVERY ENGLISH SENTENCE MUST HAVE A SURFACE SUBJECT,** that is to say, in every English sentence the subject slot must be filled by something which functions as a subject. Therefore, constructions such as the following are ungrammatical or else strictly elliptical:[7]

6. *Arrives on time every day.
[→→"He/She/It arrives on time every day."]
7. *Seems strange that he knows so much.
[→→ "It seems strange that he knows so much."]
8. *Looks like it is going to rain.
[→→ "It looks like it is going to rain."]

Why, however, should the word it and not, say, one, he, or some other person-marked form be what English uses to fill the otherwise subjectless surface slot? In part, this question answers itself: a person-marked form (which it is not) presumes a noun that is + human, and sentences 2, 6, 7 and 8 do not contain one. The other problem of course is that sentences like 2/6/7/8 contain no plausible noun, clause, or whole-sentence antecedent whatsoever. In effect, then, linguists have had to invent or presuppose an antecedent for it. Several possible it antecedents have been proposed for our syntactically necessary but semantically slippery it, among them the weather, the temperature, the time, the space, the environment, etc. Thus it is not too difficult to impose a "weather" antecedent on the it that appears in a sentence like the following, awkward or redundant though it may be:

9. I heard on the news that it sure is going to be cold today. (= "I heard on the news that the weather sure is going to be cold today.")

There as Referential, There as Non-Referential

In a general sense, what applies to it applies as well to there, though non-referential there can be used in a wider variety of situations than can its it counterpart. Let us first demonstrate the difference between referential and non-referential there:

REFERENTIAL THERE
1. Did you happen to notice my chemistry book when you

were in the clubhouse? I'm sure I left it there.

prepositional phrase expressing location	pro-prepositional phrase (location)

co-referentiality

vs. NON-REFERENTIAL THERE
2. Did you happen to notice my chemistry book when you

were in the clubhouse? There isn't any other place

prepositional phrase expressing location	non-referential there NOT expressing location

I could have left it.

NO co-referentiality

While there in #1 is clearly co-referential with in the clubhouse, there in #2 is co-referential with no possible antecedent—not with in the clubhouse, not with chemistry book, not with you, etc. There in #2, then, is non-referential. As a non-referential, this kind of there must be given a name of its own. The name most typically used is **"existential there"** because non-referential there is often used to express the existence of something, as in the following sentences:

EXISTENTIAL THERE:

> 3. There may not be a Santa Claus, but there surely is a Devil.

This sentence's there + BE construction lends itself to the following **existential paraphrase**:

> "A Santa Claus may not exist, but a Devil surely does."

> 4. There are many problems to be resolved.
>
> **existential paraphrase:**
>
> "Many problems exist, and need resolving."

> 5. There is much to do before we sleep.
>
> **existential paraphrase:**
>
> "Much exists that we must do before we sleep."

> 6. There will be time enough for that tomorrow.
>
> **existential paraphrase:**
>
> "Time enough for that exists tomorrow."

Closely related in concept and type of paraphrase to existential there (so closely, in fact, that some dismiss the distinction) is **locational there**, which the following sentences exemplify:

> 7. There is a present for you under the tree.
>
> **locational paraphrase:**
>
> "A present for you is located under the tree."

> 8. There are hundreds of houses in that area, while just four years ago not a single one had been built.
>
> **locational paraphrase:**
>
> "Hundreds of houses are located in that area, while just four years ago not a single one had been built."

9. There was a big maple tree right here before the highway was built.

locational paraphrase:

"A big maple tree was located right here before the highway was built."

Existential/locational <u>there</u> can also be used in sentences which express **events** ("There are several elephants running around loose") or **states** ("There are three corpses buried in that cave"). It should be noted as well that several other verbs besides be—verbs such as stand, dwell, and arise—can appear with non-referential <u>there</u> to express existence, location, events, and states:

10. <u>There</u> once <u>stood</u> a farmhouse where the high school now stands.
11. <u>There</u> <u>dwell</u> several tribes of pygmies in that jungle.
12. <u>There</u> <u>arose</u> a serious problem, just when we thought we had everything solved.

(A) Identify all **referential** and all **non-referential** uses of it and there. Then classify all examples of non-referential there as to subcategory. Finally, show by means of paraphrase that each there you classify as non-referential is indeed non-referential.

1. I know that there's a fly in my soup, but I can't find it.

2. Well finally: after all this searching, there's the fly in my soup I was telling you about.

3. There is where I found it, after looking everywhere.

4. It's a long long way to Tipperary, it's a long way to go.

5. They say that it's located a long long way from Tipperary.

6. As long as there are songs to sing, I'll be loving you.

7. I knew it would start to rain the minute it clouded over.

8. The minute I saw the dragon, I knew it would be breathing fire all over town.

9. He said that there were thousands of rats there.

10. It's been heard here, and there, and all around the town.

11. Sam told me there was a mouse running around the basement.

12. There just has to be some decency left in the world!

13. It ain't over til the fat lady sings.

14. Now there's just no reason in the world why you can't stay right there until I finish it.

15. It says right there in the contract that it's never too late to get your money back.

(B) Write two original sentences corresponding to each of the following descriptions.

1. non-referential it, weather antecedent

2. referential there

3. referential i̲t

4. non-referential t̲h̲e̲r̲e̲, existential/locational

5. non-referential i̲t and non-referential t̲h̲e̲r̲e̲

6. referential i̲t and referential t̲h̲e̲r̲e̲

Emphasis: Fronting for Emphasis, Clefting for Emphasis

There are several ways to express and assign emphasis (see for example pp. 95–96). One way is to place the strongest stress in the sentence on the element you wish to emphasize. Here is an example sentence to practice with:

1. Jerry murdered his great-grandfather with an axe on Thursday.
   1   **2**   **3**   **4**   **5**   **6**   **7**

By strong-stressing numbered element 1 (Jerry), we can emphasize the point that it was Jerry and not someone else who did the deed; by strong-stressing 2 (murdered), we make it clear that Jerry didn't just give his victim a friendly tap on the head; if element 3 is strong-stressed, we emphasize that it was his great-grandfather (and not someone else's) whom he murdered; and on and on, for a total of seven possibilities. Once again, strong stress achieves one of the following purposes: to contrast X with Y, or to emphasize X (sometimes at the expense of Y).

Another way to express emphasis is to "front" any noun, noun phrase, or noun-containing prepositional phrase that you wish to emphasize or contrast. By **fronting** we mean putting at the front of the sentence the element to be emphasized. There are two ways of doing this:

(1) actually **fronting** the element (without making any other changes in the word order of the sentence or in the nature of its constituent elements), or

(2) **clefting** the element, to do which involves making word-order changes and utilizing one of two special syntactic patterns: it-clefting, or wh-clefting.

Here are several examples of **fronting for emphasis**. (Strong-stressed syllables are given in bold type under acute accent marks. The fronted element is underlined in its entirety. Strong-stressing and fronting are mutually reinforcive.)

1. His great-**gránd**father Jerry murdered with an axe on Thursday.
2. On **Thúrs**day Jerry murdered his great-grandfather with an axe.
3. With an **áxe** Jerry murdered his great-grandfather on Thursday.

What follow now are several examples of **clefting**, a process which is described in detail after the examples are given:

4. It was his great-grandfather who Jerry murdered with an axe on Thursday.
Who Jerry murdered with an axe on Thursday was his great-grandfather.

5. It was on Thursday when Jerry murdered his great-grandfather with an axe. When Jerry murdered his great-grandfather with an axe was on Thursday.
6. It was with an axe that Jerry murdered his great-grandfather on Thursday. What Jerry murdered his great-grandfather with on Thursday was an axe.

As exemplified above, **clefting for emphasis** follows two distinct syntactic patterns: (1) **it-clefting,** and (2) **wh-clefting.**

In sentences that utilize **it-clefting,** the syntactic pattern is this:

It + BE + **emphasized element + relative pronoun** . . .

The it of an it-clefted sentence is non-referential.

Here are some examples of **it-clefting:**

It + was +   on Thursday + when [Jerry murdered his great-
it BE emph.element rel pro grandfather with an axe].

It + was + Jerry + who [murdered his great-grandfather with an axe on Thursday].

It + was + his great-grandfather + that [Jerry murdered with an axe on Thursday].

In sentences that utilize **wh-clefting,** the syntactic pattern is one in which the relative pronoun (wh-) appears at the very beginning of the sentence and the emphasized element at the very end:

Wh- + ... + **[emphasized element].**

Here are some examples:

When Jerry murdered his great-grandfather with an axe was on Thursday.
Who murdered his great-grandfather with an axe on Thursday was Jerry.
[It should be noted that sentences like these may sound some- what unnatural. A more natural way to say this sentence might be: "The person/The one who murdered his great-grandfather with an axe on Thursday was Jerry."]
What Jerry murdered his great-grandfather with on Thursday was an axe.

We now present the full range of clefts for a typical short sentence.

1. John gave Marsha the keys.

it- clefting:

John-emphasis:

1.a. It was John who gave Marsha the keys.

Marsha-emphasis:

1.b. It was Marsha who(m) John gave the keys to.
It was Marsha to whom John gave the keys.

keys-emphasis:

1.c. It was the keys that John gave Marsha.

wh-clefting:

John-emphasis:

1.d. Who gave Marsha the keys was John.
The person/The one who gave Marsha the keys was John.

Marsha-emphasis:

1.e. Who(m) John gave the keys to was Marsha.

keys-emphasis:

1.f. What John gave Marsha was the keys.

Note that verbs and verb phrases can neither be fronted nor clefted in standard English, thus:

*It was gave that Marsha did to John the keys.

EXERCISE 7.3

(A) First, tell which of the following sentences are clefts. (Some of these sentences are **not** clefts.) Then indicate which clefting pattern the sentence follows. Finally, de-cleft all clefts, returning each cleft sentence to its original pre-cleft syntax.

   1. Who turned out to be the murderer was Jerry.

   2. It was the glass on the floor that bothered John.

   3. It was time to go home.

   4. The drunk hid the bourbon in the cellar.

   5. What bothered John was the glass on the floor.

6. It was the thief who bit the dog, and not vice-versa.

7. It was a dark and stormy night, and a fire burned fiercely in the fireplace.

8. Where I'm going is home.

9. Where do you want to go?

10. There is nothing for us to get so upset about.

11. It's a pencil (and not a pen) that Mary needs to finish her project with.

12. Where he died doesn't interest me.

13. What doesn't interest me is where he died.

14. Who she poisoned is who we're looking for, as this is a typical case of a murder without a corpse.

15. Who she poisoned has nothing to do with the matter at hand.

(B) From each of the following, create all possible cleft sentences that involve it- clefting as well as wh-clefting.

    1. Connie stabbed Bea with a knife in the kitchen on Saturday at six after returning from the library.

    2. Ana bought Lynn a new chair with the money from the inheritance.

    3. Everyone knows the trouble I've seen.

    4. The quick brown fox jumped over the lazy sleeping dog.

    5. Henry made Joe a peanut butter and jelly sandwich.

6. Uncle Andrew gave him three new Italian sport coats for his birthday.

7. Julia spilled the bérnaise sauce on the floor in front of all the television cameras.

8. I want you to deliver a million dollars in a suitcase to my godfather by tomorrow night.

8

COMPOUND SENTENCES: COORDINATION, SUBORDINATION

Compound Sentences

Any English sentence is a **compound sentence** if it consists of two clauses or more, each of which can break off into its own separate independent sentence. Here are several examples of **compound sentences** and of the **independent sentences** they can form:

1. **[compound]** I went to bed and I fell asleep.
   [independent sentences]

   > I went to bed.
   > I fell asleep.

2. **[compound]** They made a profit but they still went under.
   [independent sentences]

   > They made a profit.
   > They still went under.

3. **[compound]** It began to rain when the sun was shining.
   [independent sentences]

   > It began to rain.
   > The sun was still shining.

4. **[compound]** He wanted me to arrive early.
   [independent sentences]

   > He wanted [something].
   > I [should] arrive early.

Here's why these independent sentences can form separate sentences: each independent sentence constitutes a clause and, as such, has its own subject and its own verb phrase.

The category **"compound sentences"** consists of two subcategories: **coordinate sentences** and **subordinate sentences**. The differences between these two subcategories are explained in detail in this chapter. For the

277

moment it's enough to say that a **coordinate sentence** contains two or more clauses of equal importance which are "coordinated" with each other by a conjunction, while a **subordinate sentence** is divided into a **main clause** and a **subordinate clause** according to the relative importance that can be assigned each one. (In very simple terms, the main clause controls the subordinate clause, and is linked to it by a conjunction.)

Coordinate Sentences

Coordinate sentences consist of two or more clauses that are "coordinated" (linked together) by any one of these conjunctions:

and   or   nor   but   for   yet

Here are some examples of coordinate sentences that use the conjunctions and, or, nor, but, for, and yet:

1. Perry paid the rent and Bill paid for the groceries.
2. Carol rode side-saddle but Pat rode astride.
3. Herman has just made his last purchase, for he has lost all his credit cards.
4. I never met the man, yet he looks so familiar.
5. I'll do it or I'll die trying.
6. Jack doesn't want to play tennis, nor does Jill want to go swimming.

Because these six sentences are compounds, each separate clause can stand apart as an independent sentence, as the following will show:

1.a. Perry paid the rent.
 b. Bill paid for the groceries.
2.a. Carol rode side-saddle.
 b. Pat rode astride.
3.a. Herman just made his last purchase.
 b. [Herman] has lost all his credit cards.
4.a. I never met the man.
 b. He looks so familiar.

One of the chief traits of **coordinate sentences** is that **their clauses can NOT participate in intra-sentential movement**. Intra-sentential movement means "movement within a sentence" and involves a change like this: A B → B A ("a sentence where A came first and B came second will change to become a sentence where B comes first and A comes second"). Coordinate sentences do not allow that kind of intra-sentential movement, as the following examples show:

5. *And Bill paid for the groceries, Perry paid the rent.
6. *But Pat rode astride, Carol rode side-saddle.
7. *For he has lost all his credit cards, Herman just made his last purchase.
8. *Yet he looks so familiar, I never met the man.
9. *Or I'll die trying, I'll do it.
10. *Nor does Jill want to go swimming, Jack doesn't want to play tennis.

It turns out that while coordinate sentences don't allow such movement, **subordinate** sentences **do**, as is illustrated by the following examples, which employ the **subordinating conjunctions** when, although, while, and because (of):

11. Larry laughed when Gustavo snorted. →
    When Gustavo snorted, Larry laughed.
12. Carol rode side-saddle although Pat rode astride. →
    Although Pat rode astride, Carol rode side-saddle.
13. Jack doesn't want to play tennis, while Jill doesn't want to go swimming. →
    While Jill doesn't want to go swimming, Jack doesn't want to play tennis.
14. The big bad wolf couldn't blow the house down because of the hurricane. →
    Because of the hurricane, the big bad wolf couldn't blow the house down.

As we already know, the six **coordinating conjunctions** are and/or/nor and but/yet/for. These six are subclassified according to their functions. The conjunctions and, or, and nor **can link more than two clauses**, whereas but, for, and yet cannot. Here is proof:

Linking TWO OR MORE clauses (and/or/nor):

15. Mrs. Schnabel does the laundry and Mr. Schnabel does the dishes and Joey makes the beds and Julie cleans the house.
16. Either Uncle Rick tells me the news or Aunt Sandy lets me know what's happening or Cousin Chuck keeps me up to date.

Linking TWO CLAUSES ONLY (but/for/yet):

17. Mary loves falafel but hates tofu.
18. *Mary loves falafel but hates tofu but can't stand eggplant.
19. The clown walks a tightrope yet gets nervous driving a car.
20. *The clown walks a tightrope yet gets nervous driving a car yet is afraid of airplanes.

Here's a consequence of the fact that but/for/yet cannot link more than two clauses: in coordinate sentences with more than two clauses, but/for/yet can only initiate the **final** clause, thus:

21. Mary hates tofu and eggplant **BUT** loves falafel.
22. The clown gets nervous driving a car and is afraid of airplanes **YET** walks a tightrope.

Coordinate sentences typically **economize by deleting redundant information** from the second clause (or subsequent clauses), thus creating **ellipses**. Examples follow. (The deleted information appears in brackets, and all the added pro-words are underlined.)

23. Mary loves falafel but [Mary] hates tofu.
24. Harry has been trying to build a neutron bomb, and Jack has [been trying to build a neutron bomb], too.
25. Harry has been trying to build a neutron bomb, and so has Jack [been trying to build a neutron bomb].
26. Harry hasn't been trying to build a neutron bomb, and neither has Jack [been trying to build a neutron bomb].
27. Harry hasn't been trying to build a neutron bomb, and Jack hasn't [been trying to build a neutron bomb] either.
28. Mrs. Schnabel does the laundry, Mr. Schnabel [does] the dishes, Joey [does] the windows, and Julie [does] the house cleaning.

In a coordinate sentence, which clause goes first? In many coordinate sentences, any one of the several clauses can go first, second, third, or anywhere, as the following will show:

29.a. Marilyn will bring the salad and Ken will bring the wine and Geri will bring the dessert.
  b. Ken will bring the wine and Marilyn will bring the salad and Geri will bring the dessert.
  c. Geri will bring the dessert and Ken will bring the wine and Marilyn will bring the salad.
30.a. Sam will wash the dishes or John will.
  b. John will wash the dishes or Sam will.

In other coordinate sentences, however, there are **logical constraints** on the order in which the various clauses can appear. Observe what happens when the clauses are switched in the following sentences:

31.a. You'll do it right or I'll punch you in the nose.
  b. *I'll punch you in the nose or you'll do it right.
32.a. You drank infected water and you got cholera.
  b. *You got cholera and you drank infected water.

Sentences 31 and 32 show that the logical order of events in the real world will affect the syntactic order of elements in a sentence. This is true even though each of any two particular coordinate clauses has the same structure. However, this is not the case when we change coordinate sentences into their **subordinate** equivalents, as the following will show:

33.a. If you don't do it right I'll punch you in the nose.
  b. I'll punch you in the nose if you don't do it right.
34.a. Because you drank infected water you got cholera.
  b. You got cholera because you drank infected water.

(A) The following are all coordinate sentences. Divide each sentence into its (two or more) separate sentence components.

1. Leslie lay down on the sidewalk and Miriam picketed.

2. The boulder was perched perilously close to the edge of the cliff, yet it still didn't move.

3. Paulie had a permit to eat like a horse but he still refused to pig out.

4. I didn't want anything more to drink, for I was already high.

5. Either your dad will get the telegram or your mom will get the letter.

6. Neither the Western Union office delivered the telegram nor the post office delivered the letter.

7. Joyce studied the verbs and Bruce studied the nouns and Vince studied the syntactic complementation patterns.

(B) In the following coordinate sentences, write in any words or phrases that have been deleted or changed wherever deletion or change have taken place.

1. The driver saw the accident but failed to stop.

2. Julie and Frank play the trombone.

3. Julie plays in the school band and Frank does too.

4. Aunt Alice won't teach you to drive the car but Aunt Sally will.

5. Steve held his breath, ran, jumped, and landed in a pile of sawdust.

6. Pete has a white and a black '57 Chevy.

7. We arrived at the party after 8:30 and so did the Szymanskis.

8. My next-door neighbor just bought a new piano, a new stereo, and a new VCR.

9. That old grouch has absolutely no patience, nor does his wife.

10. Jerry scored twenty points, Mike eleven, and Tom three.

11. Did you write me last or I you?

12. You've got to get rid of your hamster, your snake, or your monkey.

13. I haven't, but Jackie has received a check.

14. My wife swore she would never get a permanent, but she ended up doing so after all.

(C) Using what you have just learned, describe what is wrong with the following coordinate sentences.

1. *We decided to order the third entree and looked at the menu.

2. *For I was very hungry, I ordered three blue-plate specials.

3. *The teacher will fail you, or you'll have to work harder.

4. *Yet I still couldn't make up my mind, I knew I was in trouble.

5. *But he planned to take the 3:49 bus, he didn't arrive on time.

6. *Jack sat down and walked slowly into the room.

7. *The grease kept on burning, but the cook squirted it with his fire extinguisher.

8. *Mrs. García made the tamales, Dolores made, Jesse the, and Mr. García.

Subordinate Sentences

The notion that sentences can consist of more than one clause was first presented in ch. 6, where we discussed two kinds of sentences which had more than one clause and so were compound: (1) comparative sentences ("Sally runs faster than her brother [can]"), and (2) relative clause sentences ("He knows the man [who] I saw yesterday at the bank"). These sentences are similar to the subordinate sentences we are about to discuss. Subordinate sentences' basic structures differ from the basic structures of coordinate sentences. Let's look at the differences. The basic structure of a **coordinate** sentence looks like this:

1. We had an accident and we called the police.

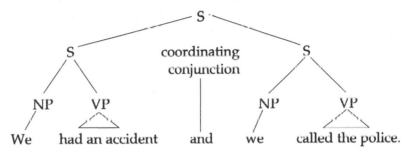

However, the basic structure of a **subordinate** sentence looks like this:

2. We had an accident before we called the police.

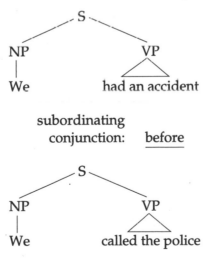

In structure # 2, the two independent sentences—"We had an accident," "We called the police"—are not viewed as having equal status: the second is subordinate to the first. On the other hand, the two independent sentences in structure # 1 **are** viewed as having equal status, for neither one is subordinate to the other. But in a subordinate sentence, one independent sentence component is taken to be the **main clause** and the other is taken to be the **subordinate clause**. The main clause is often the first clause:

3. We had an accident before we called the police.
    main clause   **subordinate clause**

However, such a syntactic arrangement is not rigid, as the following movement will show:

4. Before we called the police, we had an accident.
    subordinate clause   **main clause**

Even though the subordinate clause appears in sentence-initial position, we can still identify it as a subordinate clause because it's the clause that begins with the subordinating conjunction. There are quite a few subordinating conjunctions and they are used in a wide variety of ways. Here are a few of the more commonly used subordinating conjunctions:

as	so	although	if	even if	while	since
because	unless	when	before	after	that

Another way to determine which clause is main and which is subordinate is to ask: which is the clause that cannot appear alone exactly the way it is written? The clause that can't appear alone as written is the subordinate clause, as the following shows:

5. Before we called the police, we had an accident.
    *Before we called the police.
        (This separate sentence—*Before we called the police.—cannot stand alone as an independent proposition, though it can and does function as part of a longer narrative ["When did you take the photograph?" "Before we called the police."]; thus it constitutes the subordinate clause.)
    We had an accident.
        (This independent sentence component **can** stand alone as a separate sentence, so it's the main clause.)

One very important role that subordinate clauses play is this: subordinate clauses **complement** main clauses by adding information to them. This process is known as **sentential complementation**. Sentential complementation involves five things:

(1) sentential **adverb** complementation
(2) sentential **object** complementation; sentential **subject** complementation
(3) sentential **predicate nominative** complementation

(4) sentential **noun complement** clauses
(5) sentential **adjective complement** clauses

Let's now analyze each of these five types of complementation.

(1) Sentential <u>Adverb</u> Complementation

Subordinate clauses that function like adverbs constitute examples of sentence adverbial complementation. Here is an example:

6. We called the police <u>after we had an accident</u>.

The underlined clause answers the question "When?", a typically adverbial question. Another way to prove that the underlined clause is adverbial is to paraphrase it by using the word <u>then</u>:

We called the police <u>after we had an accident</u>.

paraphrase: We called the police then.

Here, the single-word adverb <u>then</u> successfully substitutes for the clause after we had an accident. This adverbial complement designates **time**. Sentential adverb complements can also designate **manner**—

7. <u>By the way you exaggerate everything</u>, you look like a fool.

gradation—

8. No one makes more money in a year <u>than Faisal (makes)</u>.

standpoint—

9. Epstein's defense was flawed <u>from the way the jury saw it</u>.

cause—

10. Homer can't lie <u>because his eyes always give him away</u>.

and **condition**—

11. <u>If she had saved some money</u>, she wouldn't be in this fix.

(2) Sentential Object Complementation; Sentential Subject Complementation

In this type of subordinate complementation, entire clauses function as objects or subjects. In the examples that follow, compare the "a" sentences' underlined multi-word objects and subjects with the "b" sentences' underlined one-word objects and subjects. The underlined words of the "b" sentences are the paraphrases which prove that the underlined words of the "a" sentences function as objects or subjects.

12.a. David assumes that Joe ate all the bread.
  b. David assumes <u>something</u>. = **sentential object**
13.a. I don't know <u>where poor old Uncle Zeke used to live</u>.
  b. I don't know <u>something</u>. = **sentential object**
14.a. <u>How quickly he learned that card trick</u> astounded me.
  b. <u>Something</u> astounded me. = **sentential subject**
15.a. <u>That Joe ate all the bread</u> astonished David.
  b. <u>Something</u> astonished David. = **sentential subject**
16.a. Louis said <u>that Tom knew that Gary had AIDS</u>.
  b. Louis said <u>something</u>. = **sentential object**
17.a. <u>That Tom knew that Gary had AIDS</u> shocked everyone.
  b. <u>Something</u> shocked everyone. = **sentential subject**

Notice that in sentences 16.a. and 17.a., one <u>that</u>-clause has been put inside another <u>that</u>-clause. The result looks like this in a diagram:

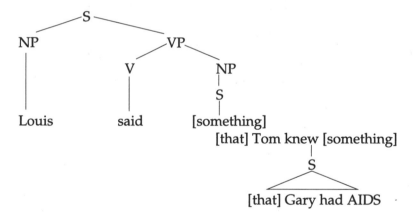

Multiple compoundings like these can go on indefinitely, as in the following:

18. Connie says that Joe said that Bea said that Carol said that Mary Gay said that Henry said that . . .

In real-world usage, of course, any hyper-compounding of this sort is limited by considerations of style and short-term memory to four or five clauses at the most.

Sentences like nos. 14, 15, and 17 above can be rewritten to begin with the dummy subject <u>it</u>:

19. It astounded me <u>how quickly he learned that card trick</u>.
20. It astonished David <u>that Joe ate all the bread</u>.
21. It shocked everyone <u>that Tom knew that Gary had AIDS</u>.

This word order is known as **extrapositional co-referentiality**. It involves adding the word it as a dummy subject, which then appears in sentence-initial position, separated by the rest of the sentence. ("Extrapositional" means that the dummy subject it is at some distance from the part of the sentence it's co-referential with.) The extrapositional co-referential it differs significantly from the it-cleft it that we discussed in ch. 7, as the following will show:

22. **[extrapositional it:]**

It astonished David that Joe ate all the bread.

   (This sentence derives from the following sentence:
   "That Joe ate all the bread astonished David.")

23. **[clefting it:]**

It was David who was astonished that Joe ate all the bread.

   (This sentence derives from the following one:
   "David was astonished that Joe ate all the bread.")

Although most sentential **subjects** can be extraposed, sentential **objects** can be extraposed only under certain conditions: (1) when the objects **occur in passive-voice constructions—**

24. It was believed by the judge that Epstein was lying.

or (2) when **delayed** objects appear in sentences with matrix verbs such as believe or perceive:

25. David believes it unlikely that Joe will eat more bread.
                                    delayed object

(3) Sentential Predicate Nominative Complementation

Subordinate clauses beginning with that can also involve predicate nominatives. In these constructions, the subject clause is linked to the predicate nominative clause by the usual copula verb be or by be plus verbs such as seem or appear. Examples:

26. The investment plan will be that you put your money in bonds.
27. The name of the game seems to be that you declare yourself innocent of all criminal intent.

(4) Sentential Noun-Complement Clauses

It is also possible for a **noun** to be complemented by a that-clause, as the following examples show:

28. The very idea that Mario took such a job was insane.
29. The notion that deficit spending doesn't matter has hurt many a nation's economy.

The *that* of sentences 28 and 29 is a complementizing conjunction and not a relative pronoun. We can prove this by attempting (and failing) to substitute other relative pronouns for *that*:

28.a. The very idea that Mario took such a job was insane.
  b. *The very idea which Mario took such a job was insane.
29.a. The notion that deficit spending doesn't matter has hurt many a nation's economy.
  b. *The notion which deficit spending doesn't matter has hurt many a nation's economy.

(5) Sentential Adjective-Complement Clauses

In these constructions, the complementizing clause refers back to an adjective, explaining it or adding more information to it. Here are some examples:

30. Richard is sad that Andrés died.
31. They were annoyed that the computer broke down.

(A) In each sentence below, identify each clause in a compound sentence, then label each clause as to the type of complemention that's involved.

1. Mary told Phillip that Dwight was writing a book.

2. Mary seemed to be glad that Lillian prevaricated.

3. That Lillian had told so many lies proved hard to believe.

4. The object of ice hockey seems to be that the players should maim each other.

5. Donna seemed to realize what was happening while Henry was telling his story.

6. It was accepted by Larry that his mother needed a nurse.

7. Jacob wrote Jessie that his ladder had been stolen.

8. How I'm supposed to lift this by myself I can't imagine.

9. The fact that you had an affair with Susie can only prove that you don't really love me after all.

10. Martha thought that she was at the fights when suddenly a hockey game broke out.

11. Sam listened to "La Bohème" while the dogs chewed on the chair in the basement.

12. Do you really believe that it's time that we free the Indianapolis 500?

13. You failed to write and you never called, but you always show up when there are Christmas presents to be had.

14. Guy said that Sandy said that Marilyn thought that the very idea that students would cheat on their comprehensive exams was shocking.

15. I tried to tell her I was happy that Fred failed Friday.

(B) Write one original sentence corresponding to each description.

1. coordinate sentence with <u>but</u>

2. coordinate sentence with <u>and</u>

3. coordinate sentence with <u>yet</u>

4. subordinate sentence with sentential adverb complementation

5. subordinate sentence with sentential object complementation

6. subordinate sentence with sentential subject complementation

7. subordinate sentence with sentential predicate nominative complementation

8. subordinate sentence with sentential noun complement clause

9. subordinate sentence with sentential adjective complement clause

10. extrapositional co-referentiality

Tenseless Complements

Infinitives and Gerunds as Tenseless Sentential Complements

In addition to the various types of clausal complementation—adverb, object, subject, predicate nominate, noun, and adjective—that we have just finished discussing, English possesses two additional types of complementation that are commonly known as **tenseless sentential complements** because they involve the two non-finite forms of the verb: the infinitive and the gerund (also known as the present participle). Here are some examples of each of these two new types of complements as contrasted with a type we have already examined, the sentential object complement:

Infinitive Complement

    1. I recommend for <u>him to arrive</u> on time.

Gerund Complement

    2. I recommend his <u>arriving</u> on time.

Sentential Object Complement: that-clause

    3. I recommend <u>that he arrive</u> on time.

These three sentences paraphrase each other; they basically mean the same thing. Each consists of two propositions: (1) I recommend [something], and (2) He [should] arrive on time. The third sentence—"I recommend that he arrive on time"—exemplifies a type of compounding we have already studied: sentential object complementation using the complementizer that; it contains two different clauses that are easily separated: "I recommend [something]" and "He [should] arrive on time." As we will learn in detail below, the first sentence ("I recommend for him to arrive on time") requires us to **change a subject pronoun (he) into an object pronoun (him)** and to use a non-finite verbal form, the infinitive (to arrive). We will also learn that the second sentence ("I recommend his arriving on time") changes a subject pronoun (he) into its corresponding possessive determiner (his) and requires a non-finite verbal form, the gerund (arriving), as its complement. Not all main-clause matrix verbs behave like recommend, which allows all three types of complementation. Some main-clause verbs **allow only sentential object "that-clause" complementation:**

    4. I believe that he leaves early.
    5. *I believe him to leave early.
    6. *I believe him leaving early.

Other main-clause verbs **allow only infinitive complements**:

7. *I let that he leave early.
8. **I let him leave early.**
9. *I let him leaving early. / *I let his leaving early.

Still other main-clause verbs **allow only gerund complements**:

10. *I flattered into that he leave early.
11. *I flattered into him leave early.
12. **I flattered him into leaving early.**

And some main-clause verbs allow two (but not three) different types of complementation: infinitive complements and gerund complements only, or that-clauses and infinitive complements only, as in the following examples:

13. **I begged that he leave early.**
14. **I begged him to leave early.**
15. *I begged him leaving early.

What is more, not all permissible types of complement sentences ellicit the same meaning, as the following will show:

16.a. **[that-clause]** Mary decided that she was sick.
  b. **[infinitive complement]** Mary decided to be sick.
17.a. **[infinitive complement]** Sandy stopped to fasten her seatbelt.
  b. **[gerund complement]** Sandy stopped fastening her seatbelt.

However, most permissible types of complement sentences do indeed ellicit the same meaning, which is why they are best presented together in the same section of a textbook.

Native speakers of English understand and produce these three types of complement sentences with little effort. But for many non-native speakers, the acquisition of a three-way complementation system can be quite a job, especially if the complementation system in their native language is much simpler or works very differently. (Spanish, for example, largely limits its complements to just one, that-clause complementation, as the following reveals:

Yo quiero que ella salga inmediatamente.
*I want that she leave immediately.
['I want her to leave immediately'])

Adding to the complexity of English complementation is the fact that there are few clear-cut over-arching generalities which apply to the hundreds of possible matrix verbs and the complementation patterns they govern. Moreover, and as we have just seen, many matrix verbs can govern different forms of complementation. While the table on pp. 306–16 provides an overview of the more important matrix verbs and the complementation patterns they take, our discussion of English complementation cannot pretend to be exhaustive, and certain details have been glossed over or omitted altogether for the sake of brevity.

We'll now examine in depth the three main patterns that English employs to express complementation: that-clauses, infinitive complements, and gerund complements.

that-Clause

That-clause complementation is located in the subordinate clause. That-clause complementation is governed by many different verbs which appear in the matrix clause, including many **verbs of persuasion** (e.g., advise, ask, demand, insist, forbid), **verbs of communication** (e.g., admit, convey, mention, report), and **verbs of knowing** (e.g., believe, know, take for granted). (A verb of persuasion is one which we use to try and persuade someone to do something: "I advised him to leave early." A verb of communication typically transmits information: "I mentioned that he was going to leave early." Verbs of knowing indicate that the speaker possesses a certain knowledge: "I believe you are going to leave early.") In most dialects of English, matrix verbs of persuasion require that the conjugated verb of the subordinate that-clause be in the subjunctive mode. This means that the verb's 3.sg. present-tense form will lack the characteristic /z/, which in modern English is effectively the only morphological difference between the indicative mode (where the /z/ is present) and the subjunctive mode (where the /z/ is absent). This difference is exemplified by the following two sentences:

1. He insists that she arrive on time. [subjunctive mode]
2. He admits that she arrives on time. [indicative mode]

Infinitive Complement

Infinitive complement constructions are divided into two subgroups according to the process that each one employs:

equi deletion—
3. Edgar expects to visit Las Vegas.

and **raising to object** (pronounced [áb–jèkt]):
4. Edgar expects her to visit Las Vegas.

Let's now examine each one of these processes separately.

EQUI DELETION

In an embedded sentence such as the one we have just seen—Edgar expects to visit Las Vegas—we find two independent sentence components:

> **(a)** Edgar expects [something].
>
> and **(b)** Edgar visits Las Vegas.

When these two single-clause sentences merge into a bi-clausal compound sentence, the finite 3.sg. present-tense verb form visits is transformed into the infinitive to visit: Edgar expects to visit . . . . It will be necessary to comment at greater length on the phenomenon known as **equi deletion**, which is illustrated by the following diagram:

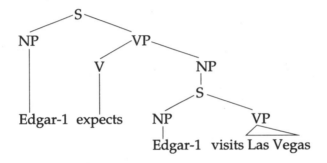

Edgar-1 is the same Edgar as Edgar-1, so we can speak of the two Edgars as being **equivalent**. As if to avoid redundancy, English deletes the second or equivalent Edgar, thereby bringing about an **equi(valent) deletion**, which we shorten to **equi deletion**. When creating this type of compound sentence, we thus perform two transformations—equi deletion, and transforming the finite verb to an infinitive—as follows:

> Edgar-1 expects Edgar-1 visits Las Vegas
> →→→ Edgar expects   to visit Las Vegas

The gap left by the deletion of the second Edgar-1 is then bridged, leaving:

> →→→ Edgar expects to visit Las Vegas.

A large number of matrix verbs—attempt, care, crave, demand, fail, long, remember, and wish—conform to the equi deletion pattern. Here are some additional examples of equi deletion:

5. Jennifer attempted to make a neutron bomb.
6. Victor didn't care to sleep in a tent.
7. Our relatives demand to inherit all the money.
8. The dog longed to be taken for a walk.

As sentence # 8 has shown, matrix verbs conforming to the equi deletion subgroup can also take passive infinitives (to be taken), whose tree diagram looks like this:

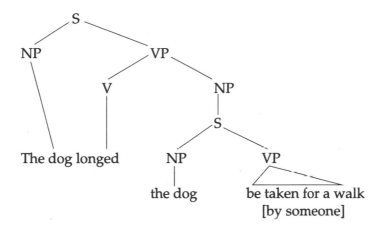

Result: "The dog longed to be taken for a walk [by someone]."

RAISING TO OBJECT

A compound sentence that is typical of this second type of infinitive complement subgroup has two independent sentence components, as the following will show:

> Edgar expects her to visit Las Vegas.
> (a) Edgar expects [something].
> (b) She visits Las Vegas.

A diagram for Edgar expects her to visit Las Vegas looks like this:

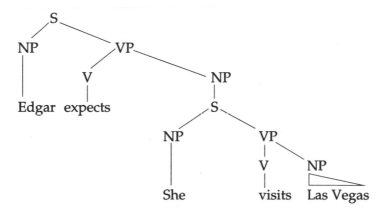

Obviously Edgar and she are not equivalent, so no equi deletion can take place here. What takes place instead is something called **subject raising to**

object, or, more briefly put, **raising to object**. The subject that raises to object is she; the object it raises to is her, as we now see:

Edgar expects [something]
                    She visits to Las Vegas
→→→ Edgar expects her to visit Las Vegas.

We call this process **raising** because of the spatial relationship between she and her in the following diagram:

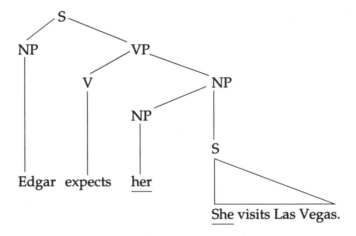

In this diagram, the subject (she) of the subordinate or "lower" sentence component is raised into the matrix or "higher" sentence component where it becomes the direct object her. Among the many matrix verbs which produce this complementation pattern are cause, like, need, prefer, and want, as the following examples show:

9. Roy wanted me to take out the garbage.
10. Judy caused Clara to throw a tantrum.
11. I always like them to arrive on time.

Some matrix verbs, such as have/hear/help/let/make, cause the infinitive-marking to to be **deleted** in this type of construction, as the following examples show:

12. They had him throw the bum out.
    (*They had him to throw the bum out.)
13. I let her drive to Las Vegas.
    (*I let her to drive to Las Vegas.)
14. The principal made me stand in the corner.
        (Compare nos. 12, 13, and 14 to sentences whose matrix verbs do not allow the deletion of the infinitive-marking to, e.g. "He forced me to stand in the corner.")

Other matrix verbs such as ask, be necessary, beg, dread, love, pray, prefer, recommend, signal, and want can prompt a **discontinuous complementizer** construction in the subordinate clause. The discontinuous complementizer consists of the words "for . . . to", as the following examples show:

15. It was necessary for him to arrive on time.
16. I just love for them to visit us.
17. The traffic cop signaled for us to stop.

Gerund Complement

Gerund complements behave like infinitive complements in that they too are divided into two subgroups according to the process that each one employs:

—**equi deletion**
  1. Joyce enjoys playing tennis.

—**raising to object**
  2. Joyce enjoys John's playing tennis.

We will now examine each of these two subgroups in greater detail.

EQUI DELETION

This subgroup is identical to the equideletion subgroup of infinitive complements in the following sense: in both, the equivalent subject of the subordinate clause is deleted:

1. Joyce enjoys playing tennis.
  –   Joyce-1 enjoys [something]
                    Joyce-1 plays tennis
  →→→ Joyce enjoys   playing tennis →
       Joyce enjoys playing tennis.

RAISING TO OBJECT (AND RAISING TO GENITIVE)

This subgroup is identical to the raising-to-object subgroup of the infinitive complement in this sense: both raise the subject of the subordinate clause to a position in which that subject functions as the object of the main clause. Here is an example:

2. Joyce enjoys his playing tennis.
  =   Joyce enjoys [something]
                    He plays tennis
  →→→ Joyce enjoys his playing tennis

The gerund—playing—effectively functions as a verbal noun, i.e., a noun which derives from a verb. (That words such as playing can function as nouns is demonstrated by sentences like these in which a determiner precedes a gerund:

—All that playing will only irritate your elbow.
—The plowing was finished by noon.
—Some singing took place after dinner.)

Note that the raised-to-object pronoun in # 2—his—appears as a possessive determiner in the **genitive case**, not the object case. His, then, is not an object the way an object-case word like him is. Consider the following sentence:

3. Edgar expects him to drive to Las Vegas.

If # 2—Joyce enjoys his playing tennis—behaved like # 3 exactly, then # 2 would have to read as follows:

4. Joyce enjoys him playing tennis.

It turns out that while prescriptive English disapproves of the use of him in # 4, colloquial English permits it. Thus native speakers regularly produce both versions of our sentence about Joyce's friend and the tennis he plays:

5.a. Joyce enjoys his playing tennis.
   b. Joyce enjoys him playing tennis.

The reason prescriptivists disapprove of usages such as 5.b. is because in some contexts the contrast between the genitive form and the object form triggers a distinction in meaning. Consider the following:

6.a. Mary dislikes the house guest's chewing tobacco.
   b. Mary dislikes the house guest chewing tobacco.

Sentence 6.a. can be paraphrased thus: "Mary dislikes the smell/ mess/health hazard created when the house guest chews tobacco." Sentence 6.b., on the other hand, can mean: "Mary dislikes the house guest, who just happens to be chewing tobacco." Thus the object of Mary's dislike in 6.b. can be interpreted to focus on the guest himself, not on his tobacco chewing, or 6.b. can serve to distinguish between various house guests, only one of whom Mary dislikes:

6.c. Mary dislikes the house guest [who is] chewing tobacco, but she adores the house guest [who is] drinking tea.

In other contexts, however, it is impossible to perceive any difference between the results of **raising to object** (him, John, etc.) and the results of **raising to genitive** (his, John's, etc.), as the following will show:

7.a. We don't like John chewing tobacco.
   b. We don't like John's chewing tobacco.

Both 7.a. and 7.b. are grammatical, though prescriptivists clearly prefer 7.b., and 7.a. does sound more colloquial. In any event, both 7.a. and 7.b. convey the same meaning.

All linguists agree that some matrix verbs prefer (or demand) that raising to **object** in gerund-complement subordinate clauses occur, while other matrix verbs prefer (or demand) that only raising to **genitive** should take place in gerund-complement subordinate clauses. Here are several examples of both phenomena, as well as of matrix verbs that show no preference and permit raising to object as well as raising to genitive in the subordinate clause:

PREFERENCE OR DEMAND FOR RAISING TO OBJECT

8. I flattered him into working from ten to six.
(Cf. *I flattered his working from ten to six.)

9. I need him working from ten to six.
(Cf. *I need his working from ten to six.)

PREFERENCE OR DEMAND FOR RAISING TO GENITIVE

10. I authorize his signing the checks.
(Cf. *I authorize him signing the checks.)

11. I enjoy his playing tennis.
(Cf. ?I enjoy him playing tennis.)

NO PREFERENCE—BOTH PHENOMENA POSSIBLE

12. I remember his earning only $9,000 a year.
13. I remember him earning only $9,000 a year.
14. I insisted on his arriving on time.
15. I insisted on him arriving on time.

TABLE 1. COMMONLY USED MATRIX VERBS AND THE COMPLEMENTATION PATTERNS THAT THEY CO-OCCUR WITH

This lengthy but not exhaustive table lists 75 English verbs that are commonly used in the matrix part of our matrix-clause-plus-subordinate-clause sentences. The table lists the nine complementation patterns discussed in this chapter, and indicates which matrix verbs co-occur ('are employed') with which pattern(s). Here is how to use this table: by reading it horizontally, one learns which matrix verb co-occurs with which complementation pattern; by reading it vertically, one learns which complementation pattern co-occurs with which matrix verb. For example, advise in the matrix co-occurs with either a that-clause complement ("I advise that she sell") or else with an infinitive complement plus raising to object ("I advise her to sell").

Excluded from this table are all matrix-plus-complementation patterns which struck us as unnatural, stilted, obsolete, obsolescent, or possibly so. (We have used the ? symbol to mark those patterns which strike us as **possibly** unnatural, obsolete, and so forth.) By employing the complement verb phrase *sing* throughout, we have sought uniformity of content to the greatest extent possible; however, the equally compelling need to achieve naturalness has prompted minor variations in tense or length on several occasions. It should also be noted that given the complexity of English complementation, not all native speakers will agree on the grammaticality of all matrix-plus-complementation patterns presented here, and some may indeed conclude that a particular pattern sounds unnatural, obsolete, etc.

Those verbs usable in the matrix clauses of compound sentences appear in bold-face type in the left-hand column of the table, thus: **admit, advise, ask, attempt** ... Numbered sentences follow each matrix verb; these numbered sentences illustrate each of the subordinate-clause patterns with which the particular matrix verb can co-occur. (Note that while some matrix verbs can co-occur with just one or two subordinate-clause patterns and others can co-occur with as many as six or seven, no matrix verb co-occurs with all nine patterns.) The numbers illustrating each pattern range from 1 through 9; the following numbered paragraphs explain each one of the subordination patterns that the matrix verbs can co-occur with:

1. The complement is a subordinate that-clause, with the clause's verb in the subjunctive. (Example: *I prefer that she sing lullabies.* [In this example, the matrix verb is **prefer** while the subordinate that-clause's verb is sing. We know it's in the subjunctive mode because the verb form lacks the characteristic 3.sg. present-tense /z/ morpheme.])

2. The complement is a subordinate that-clause, with the clause's verb in the indicative. (Example: *I know that she sings lullabies.* [In this example, the matrix verb is know while the subordinate that-clause's verb is sings. We know it's in the indicative mode because the verb form ends in the characteristic 3.sg. present-tense /z/ morpheme.])

3. The complement is an infinitive. Pattern 3 is characterized by equi deletion. (Example: *I prefer to sing.*)

4. The complement is an infinitive. Pattern 4 entails raising to object, and the infinitive's marker (the word to) is deleted in the process. (Example: *I made her sing.*)

5. The complement is an infinitive. Pattern 5 entails raising to object, and the infinitive's marker to is retained, not deleted. (Example: *I prefer her to sing lullabies.*)

6. The complement is an infinitive. Pattern 6 entails raising to object, and the infinitive marker to is complemented by the discontinuous pre-posed addition of for. (Example: *I prefer for her to sing.*)

7. The complement is a gerund. Pattern 7 is characterized by equi deletion. (Example: *I prefer singing.*)

8. The complement is a gerund. Pattern 8 entails raising to object. (Example: *I prefer him singing, not chanting.*)

9. The complement is a gerund. Pattern 9 entails raising to genitive (specifically, a possessive determiner). (Example: *I prefer his singing.*)

admit   2. I admit that she sings adequately.
7. I admit singing for hours on end.

advise   1. I advise that you sing on key.
5. I advised her to sing on key.
9. ?I advised her singing anywhere but in a nightclub.

allow ['permit']
5. I allowed her to sing endlessly.
6. ?I allowed for her to sing endlessly.
7. I allow singing in my tavern.
9. I allowed his singing to go on and on.

allow ['acknowledge']
2. I allow that she sings adequately.

ask
1. May I ask that you sing a little less loudly?
3. I only ask to sing for my supper.
5. I asked him to sing on key.
6. I asked for him to sing on key.

attempt
3. I attempted to sing, but failed.
7. I attempted singing, but failed.

authorize

> 5. I authorized them to sing at the concert.
> 9. I authorized their singing at the concert.

avoid

> 7. I avoid singing like the plague.
> 9. I avoid her singing whenever I possibly can.

be:

[it] **be** [noun or adjective of suasion or emotional commentary]:

be a pleasure

> 3. It'd be a pleasure to sing.
> 6. It'd be a pleasure for her to sing.

be awful

> 2. It's awful that she sings for her supper.
> 3. It's awful to sing in front of such an audience.
> 6. It's awful for her to sing in front of those people.

be desirable

> 1. It's desirable that he sing classical music.
> 3. It's desirable to sing in Carnegie Hall.
> 6. It's desirable for him to sing at least twice a day.

be essential

> 1. It's essential that he sing classical music.
> 3. It's essential to sing at the Met at least once.
> 6. It's essential for her to sing Bach cantatas.

be important

> 1. It's important that she sing a song of six pence.
> 3. It's important to sing from early childhood onward.
> 6. It's essential for her to sing on key for a change.

be necessary

> 1. It's necessary that he sing along with Mitch.
> 3. It's necessary to sing sweet songs of love.
> 6. It's necessary for him to sing as fast as he can.

be nice

> 2. It's nice that she sings so loud and clear.
> 3. It's nice to sing before such a great crowd tonight.
> 6. It's nice for her to sing when I play the piano

be sad

    2. It was sad that he sang so poorly.
    3. It was sad to sing so poorly before so many people.
    6. It was sad for him to sing like a sick cow in heat.

[sub.pr.] **be afraid**

    2. I am afraid that she sings terribly.
    3. I am afraid to sing a Wagner aria.
    6. I am afraid for her to sing at the recital.

be determined ('insistent')
    1. We were determined that he sing the song again.
    3. We were determined to sing.
    6. We were determined for him to sing the song again.

be eager
    1. They are eager that he sing like an angel.
    3. They are eager to sing like angels.
    6. They are eager for him to sing like an angel.

be happy
    2. They are happy that she sings like Cecilia Bartoli.
    3. She is happy to sing like Cecilia Bartoli.
    6. They are happy for her to sing like Cecilia Bartoli.

be insistent
    1. You are insistent that she sing on key.

beg

    1. I begged that she sing a silly song.
    3. I begged to sing a silly song.
    5. I begged her to sing a silly song.
    6. I begged for her to sing a silly song.

believe

    2. I believe that he sings off key.
    5. I believe him to sing off key.

care

    2. I care that she sings enormously well.
    3. She always cared enough to sing enormously well.
    6. I cared for her to sing enormously well.

cause

    5. We caused him to sing off key.
    6. By our actions, we caused singing to happen.
    9. We caused his singing to happen.

command

    1. ?I command that she sing about the Easter bunny.

    5. I command her to sing about the Easter bunny.

compel

    5. I compelled him to sing.

convince

    5. They convinced her to sing.

crave

    1. I crave that he sing.

    3. I crave to sing at the Met.

    6. I crave for him to sing so sweetly.

    7. I crave singing and dancing.

    9. I crave his singing.

decree ('order')

    1. I decree that she sing for her supper.

demand

    1. We demand that he sing "O sole mio."

    3. We demand to sing "O sole mio."

    6. We demand for him to sing "O sole mio."

deprive . . . of

    8. They deprived him of singing for seven whole months.

desire

    1. They desired that he sing.

    3. They desired to sing.

    5. They desired him to sing.

    7. They desired singing at their wedding.

    9. They desired his singing at their wedding.

determine ('decree')

    1. I determined that she sing in public.

dread

    6. I dreaded for him to sing.

    7. I dread singing.

    8. I dreaded him singing the national anthem.

    9. I dread his singing most of all.

drive ('impel, force')

    5. They drove her to sing for hours on end.

encourage

    5. We encouraged him to sing at the corner bar.

    7. We encouraged singing at the corner bar.

    9. We encouraged his singing at the corner bar.

enjoy

    6. They enjoyed for him to sing at top volume.

    7. They enjoyed singing at top volume.

    8. They enjoyed him singing at top volume.

    9. They enjoyed his singing at top volume.

entice

    5. I enticed her to sing.

expect ('wish'; cf. 'assume')

    2. We expect that she sings beautifully.

    3. We expect to sing at the country club next year.

    5. We expect her to sing at the country club next year.

    6. We expect for her to sing at the country club.

    7. We expect singing at the country club.

fail

    3. We always fail to sing on key.

flatter . . . into

    8. I flattered him into singing "O sole mio."

forbid

    1. I forbade that he sing in Ruthenian.

    5. I forbid him to sing in Ruthenian.

    7. I forbade singing in Ruthenian.

    8. I forbid him singing in Ruthenian.

    9. I forbid his singing in Ruthenian.

force

    5. I forced him to sing in Hungarian.

    9. I forced his singing in Hungarian.

have ('obligate')

    4. We had her sing all night long.

    8. We had her singing all night long.

hear ('to be given to understand')

    2. They heard that he sings old Sinatra songs.

hear ('to perceive aurally')

    4. They heard him sing old Sinatra songs.

    7. They heard singing from inside the corner bar.

    8. They heard him singing inside the corner bar.

    9. They heard his singing inside the corner bar.

help

    3. Every week they help to sing in the choir.

    4. They helped her sing in the choir.

    5. They helped her to sing in the choir.

hint

    1. I hinted that she sing at least one song.

    2. I hinted that she sings quite nicely.

    6. I hinted for her to sing.

imply

    2. I implied that she sings quite nicely.

induce

    5. They induced him to sing just one more song.

influence

    5. We influenced him to sing in the key of B flat.

    9. We influenced his singing in the key of B flat.

insist ('command')

    1. I insist that she sing at the top of her lungs.

    6. I insist for her to sing at the top of her lungs.

insist on

    7. They insisted on singing all night.

    8. They insisted on him singing all night.

    9. They insisted on his singing all night.

know

    2. I know that she sings on Sundays.

    5. I know her to sing on Sundays.

    6. ?I know for her to sing on Sundays.

    7. I know singing.

    9. I know his singing.

lead

    5. We always lead her to sing.

let

    4. We let her sing whenever she wants to.

like

    3. I like to sing.

    5. I like him to sing.

    6. I like for him to sing.

    7. I like singing.

    8. I used to like him singing all day long.

    9. I used to like his singing all day long.

long

    3. I long to sing falsetto.

    6. I long for her to sing basso profundo.

love

    3. We love to sing old work songs.

    5. We love her to sing old work songs.

    6. We love for her to sing.

    7. We love singing.

    8. We love him singing.

    9. We love his singing.

make ('obligate')

    4. I made her sing.

mention

    2. I mentioned that he sings.

    7. I mentioned singing.

    9. I mentioned his singing.

move ('propose a course of action')

    1. I move that she sing an aria.

    6. I moved for her to sing an aria.

need

    3. I need to sing scales to keep in practice.

    5. I need him to sing scales to keep in practice.

    6. I need for him to sing scales to keep in practice.

    7. I need singing in my life.

    8. I need him singing in my life.

    9. I need his singing in my life.

obligate

    5. I obligated him to sing for seven hours.

    9. ?I obligated his singing for seven hours.

order

1. I order that she sing.
5. I ordered her to sing.
6. I ordered for her to sing.
7. I ordered singing, not violin playing.
9. ?I ordered her singing, not her playing the violin.

permit

5. They permitted him to sing.
7. They permitted singing.
8. ?They permitted him singing.
9. They permitted his singing.

persuade

5. We persuaded her to sing one final song.

pray

1. We pray that she sing on key.
3. We prayed to sing at her wedding.
6. We prayed for her to sing on key.

prefer

1. I prefer that she sing opera.
3. I prefer to sing, not chant.
5. I prefer her to sing opera.
6. I prefer for her to sing opera.
7. I prefer singing.
8. I prefer him singing Brahms, not Schubert.
9. I prefer his singing ragtime, not jazz.

prevent [. . . from]

7. I prevent singing whenever I can.
8. I prevented him from singing last night.
9. I prevented his singing last night.

propose

1. I propose that she sing another round.
3. I propose to sing another round.
5. I propose her to sing another round.
6. I propose for her to sing another round.
7. I propose singing one more round.
8. I propose him singing one more round.
9. I propose his singing one more round.

recommend

    1. They recommend that we sing.
    6. They recommend for us to sing.
    7. They recommend singing.
    9. They recommend our singing.

remind

    2. They reminded [us] that she sings beautifully.
    5. They reminded her to sing.

report

    2. I can report that he sings wonderfully.
    7. The cops reported singing at 3 p.m. in a dark alley.
    8. The cops reported him singing too loud at that hour.
    9. The cops reported his singing too loud at that hour.

request

    1. I request that you sing along.
    3. I request to sing.
    5. I requested her to sing, but she wouldn't.
    6. I requested for her to sing, but she wouldn't.
    7. I requested singing.
    9. I requested her singing, but she refused.

require

    1. They required that we sing.
    3. They required to sing.
    5. They required us to sing.
    6. ?They required for us to sing.
    7. They required singing.
    8. ?They required us singing.
    9. They required our singing.

rule

    1. The court ruled that he sing.
    6. The court ruled for him to sing.

signal

    2. I signaled to the awaiting masses that I sing well.
    5. I signaled her to sing.
    6. I signaled for her to sing.

stipulate

    1. They stipulated that we sing to work off our penalty.
    6. ?They stipulated for us to sing.

7. They stipulated singing, not yodeling.
9. They stipulated our singing, not our yodeling.

suggest ('mildly command'; cf. 'venture an opinion')
1. I suggested that she sing.
6. I suggest for her to sing.
7. I suggest singing.
9. I suggest her singing.

tempt
5. Jeffrey tempted him to order another dessert.

trick . . . into
8. Jeffrey tricked him into ordering another dessert.

urge
1. We urge that she sing in tune.
5. We urge her to sing in tune.

want
3. They want to sing.
5. They want him to sing.
6. They want for him to sing.
8. They want him singing.
9. They want his singing.

warn ('urge threateningly'; cf. 'inform threateningly')
5. They warned her not to sing.
6. They warned for her not to sing.

wish
3. I wish to sing right now.
5. I wish him to sing right now.
6. I wished for him to sing immediately.

Purpose Complements

A purpose complement is an infinitive which answers the question "Why?" and thus functions like an adverb. Here are some examples:

16. Tubby lives to eat.
17. Costas swims to stay fit.

Purpose-complement infinitives do **not** function like the noun-phrase infinitives we have been examining so far in this chapter, as the following will show:

Tubby lives to eat   **[purpose complement]**
/= *Tubby lives [something]
Cf. Edgar expects to drive   **[noun-phrase infinitive]**
= Edgar expects [something]

Purpose complements can also be expressed by means of gerunds—

18. They sold donuts for the purpose of <u>helping</u> the fund drive.

and by means of <u>so</u> that-clauses:

19. They sold donuts <u>so that</u> they could help the fund drive.

Miscellaneous Complementation Patterns

The following two sentences though superficially similar have very different underlying structures:

20. He is eager to please.
21. He is easy to please.

Sentence 20 states that the subject is eager to please someone, while #21 indicates that it is easy for someone to please him. Sentence 20 is reminiscent of (though not identical to) the infinitive-complement constructions we examined above:

Edgar expects to drive to Las Vegas.
= Edgar expects to [drive somewhere]
He is eager to please.
= He is eager to [please someone]

Sentence 21, on the other hand, reminds us somewhat of the passive infinitive-complement construction we examined above:

The dog longs to be taken for a walk.
= The dog longs to be [taken somewhere by someone]
He is easy to please.
= It is easy [for him] to be [pleased by someone]

SUMMARY OF ALL THE ABOVE SENTENTIAL COMPLEMENTATION PATTERNS

<u>that</u>-clauses:

He insists that she leave on time.
He knows that she leaves on time.

infinitive complements:

> **equi deletion:**
>
>> Edgar expects to visit Las Vegas.
>
> **raising to object:**
>
>> Edgar expects her to visit Las Vegas.

gerund complements:

> **equi deletion:**
>
>> Joyce enjoys playing tennis.
>
> **raising to object:**
>
>> I kept him working until ten o'clock.
>
> **raising to genitive/possessive determiner:**
>
>> I really enjoy his playing.

purpose complements:

> Tubby lives to eat.

miscellaneous complements:

>> He is eager to please.
>> He is easy to please.

EXERCISE 8.3

(A) Underline and then label all sentential complement patterns in the examples below. (Underline the matrix clause just once, and then underline the subordinate clause[s] twice.)

1. Armando wanted Marilyn to fall in love with Vince.

2. The customer convinced the clerk to give her a discount.

3. Harry's wife stopped him from smoking in bed.

4. I don't believe that you forgot to pay the rent.

5. I want to live.

6. The guru said he would pray for her to get well.

7. Vince avoided buying a computer until 1992.

8. Isn't there some way to prevent Joe from eating all the bread?

9. They elected her to be president of the club.

10. He absolutely forbids their giving away any more money.

11. All seven patriarchs have suggested that you stop acting in such a Byzantine fashion.

12. Does your wife mind you smoking in the house?

13. Does your wife mind your smoking in the house?

14. The police don't recommend her walking alone at night.

15. The man motioned for us to drive around the disabled car.

16. Heinrich didn't care to be pushed around by his classmates.

17. The angry coach made the team run four laps around the track.

18. It's important for you to be there on time.

19. Zeke forced Abner to drink some of his white lightning.

20. Despite the pain in his back, Phillip kept on removing weeds.

21. Mr. Smith doesn't like his wife's constant snoring.

22. We flattered the pianist into playing another sonata.

23. Maude enjoys having her back scratched.

24. The hitchhiker ordered Edgar to drive her to Las Vegas.

(B) Write two original sentences corresponding to each of the following descriptions.

1. that-clause

2. purpose complement

3. infinitive complement equi deletion

4. infinitive complement raising to object

5. gerund complement equi deletion

      6. gerund complement raising to object

(C) Some of the sentences below exhibit one pattern of complementation but could just as well convey the same meaning through a different pattern of complementation. If possible, rewrite each of the sentences below, using any different pattern of complementation which preserves the meaning of the original. Label the pattern that appears in print as well as the pattern you have written down.

      1. It's urgent that she call her answering service.

      2. Did the principal make Bart stay after school again?

      3. I dared them to jump off the top of the Sears Tower.

      4. The judge considered the witness to be lying.

      5. We intend for them to pay us what they owe.

      6. England expects every man to do his duty!

      7. They said for us to take off our shoes at the door.

      8. Why do you urge that she become a psychiatrist?

9. John loves dancing the foxtrot.

10. She hates it that her husband bathes the dog in the kitchen.

11. I expressly forbid her leaving school before she turns 14.

12. What did you instruct us to do today?

13. The cheerleaders prayed for their team to win.

14. We had hoped that you would visit us this summer.

15. An understanding classmate helped Henry learn Ancient Aramaic.

16. Dirk saw the Nazis coming down the street.

17. The family prefers that Tiffany buy a new pair of topsiders.

18. Helga said she would give her right arm to be ambidextrous.

19. Did you remember that you owed me $1,000?

20. Jeff tempted Richard to order another dessert.

(D) Determine whether there is any difference in meaning between each of the following complementized pairs, then explain what that difference consists of.

1.a. Harvey remembered to lock the door.
  b. Harvey remembered locking the door.

2.a. Mabel heard Cecilia Bartoli sing.
  b. Mabel heard Cecilia Bartoli singing.

3.a. The colonel advised that the soldier be court-martialed.
  b. The colonel advised the soldier to be court-martialed.

4.a. Julius neglected to study.
  b. Julius neglected studying.

5.a. Ms. Hendrix admires the man's singing.
  b. Ms. Hendrix admires the man singing.

6.a. Would the hostess mind our bringing our own wine?
  b. Would the hostess mind us bringing our own wine?

(E) The following two sentences reveal a similar word order but manifest semantically different matrix verbs and unquestionably different underlying structures. Explain the difference between the two sentences in underlying structure and in meaning, using diagrams if you find them useful.

    (a) We persuaded him to pay for the tickets.
    (b) We promised him to pay for the tickets.

NOTES

1. There are widespread regional differences in the standard American English pronunciation of this word: some—chiefly northern—pronounce catch [kɛč], while others—chiefly midlands and southern—pronounce it [kæč]. Both forms are generally accepted. However, a third American pronunciation—[kɪč]—is considered unacceptable by most speakers.

2. Two rival standard pronunciations typify this form also: [kɔt]—chiefly northern, midwestern, and southern—and [kat] (mainly Californian but also midlands and western to some extent). The [ɔ] → [a] shift has been going on in all dialects of English for centuries, and in some dialects has all but eradicated [ɔ] except in a limited number of phonetic environments.

3. The word "conditional" appears between quotation marks because while the **forms** under consideration here are conditional, their **functions** are not. For a thorough discussion of what constitutes conditionality, see the appropriate section at the end of ch. 4. For a continuing discussion of the various functions that the forms of the conditional—both synthetic and periphrastic—are employed to represent, see the present chapter.

4. This statement is true of American English only. British English typically treats main-verb <u>have</u> like <u>be</u>, i.e., as a verb which does not allow <u>do</u>-insertion; thus:

+	I have a dog.
−	I haven't a dog.
yn+	Have I a dog?
yn−	Haven't I a dog?
wh/co	Why have I a dog?

    Note however that in British English the wh/co has tended to take do-insertion, especially in recent years ("Why do I have a dog?"), and American English sometimes allows a do-insertionless construction such as "I haven't any money," especially if the register of discourse is formal (or if the speaker/writer is consciously imitating British usage!).

5. Strictly speaking, when, where, and why are relative **adverbs,** not relative pronouns, but since the way all seven forms function is not dissimilar, we allow ourselves this oversimplification.

6. Certain lects **do** allow the deletion of relative pronouns that constitute the subjects of their relative clauses, as in the following: "The man saw me yesterday owed me money." However, this usage is highly stigmatized.

7. There are two important exceptions to this rule: (1) unmarked imperatives ("Get in the house right this very minute!") and (2) elliptical and often very colloquial sentences from which a subject has been deleted but where a subject is still understood and therefore retrievable ("Yep, sure do like her sody pop, don't she?").

INDEX